MYSTERIES AND
INTRIGUES OF THE BIBLE

MYSTERIES

AND

INTRIGUES

OF THE

BIBLE

EXTRAORDINARY EVENTS AND FASCINATING PEOPLE

EDITED BY
JONATHAN A. MICHAELS

FAMILY
CHRISTIAN
PRESS

Truly, O God of Israel, our Savior,

you work in strange and mysterious ways.

ISAIAH 45:15

Visit Tyndale's exciting Web site at www.tyndale.com

This book was developed by The Livingstone Corporation. Project staff includes Michael Kendrick, Jonathan Farrar, Bruce Barton, Greg Asimakoupoulos, Cecil Cole, Kari Barton, Betsy Elliot, Steve Hawkins, Mark Fackler, Amy Ronne, Randy Southern, and Neil Wilson.

ISBN 0-8423-5142-6

Printed in the United States of America

05 04 03 02 01 00 99 98
10   9   8   7   6   5   4

CONTENTS

INTRODUCTION

The Mysteries of the Bible

The Bible has been with us for nearly two thousand years, and the early books of the Old Testament have existed almost twice that long. Its enduring life attests not only to its great spiritual treasures but also to its amazing stories, astonishing miracles, and intriguing facts that continue to grip readers today. *Mysteries and Intrigues of the Bible* simply retells those stories in a fast-paced format. Its concise organization allows readers to enjoy as much as they want in the amount of time available to them.

Despite its extraordinary and sometimes lighthearted tone, *Mysteries and Intrigues of the Bible* seeks to uphold the value of Scripture. Even today, the modern scholar or scientist is hard-pressed to provide a logical, natural explanation for the events described in the Bible. We must rely on the Bible authors' interpretations to shed light on otherwise inconceivable happenings. Their confident understanding of these events points us beyond ourselves to consider the One who created all things.

Each chapter in this book presents these amazing stories in a variety of ways. "Strange but True" investigates unusual stories in a thought-provoking style. "Curious Connections" brings together a series of related events that all share a puzzling or astonishing similarity. "FAQs" (Frequently Asked Questions) answers common questions about the supernatural or miraculous. "Did You Know?" presents unusual facts about the Bible. Finally, the charts and lists further demonstrate the wonders of the Bible in a wide context, taking in the sweep of Scripture.

Scripture references are provided with each feature for the reader who wants to examine the facts further. In fact, we would encourage you to reread these Bible passages to grasp the full impact of God's work among his people. We hope you enjoy the wonders described in this book and pause to consider the great truths they point to.

ONE

BAFFLING BEHAVIOR

Strange and Inexplicable Deeds

Crimson Tide

What caused a sudden catastrophe in the Nile River?

On a hot day in the tropics, people will swim in pretty brackish water—anything to cool off. But on this day in Egypt, bathers scampered out of the water as if they had seen a shark. And well they might have wondered if sharks were not invading their great Nile River, for its waters had suddenly turned bloodred.

The Nile is a big river. It stretches 4,160 miles from central Uganda to the Mediterranean Sea. Nine countries share its basin of 1,150,000 square miles. That's a lot of water, but it was more than H_2O the day Moses went to Pharaoh demanding that the Hebrew slaves be freed.

For 400 years, the descendants of Jacob had lived in Egypt, first as guests but eventually as unpaid workers roughly handled by the powerful Egyptian Dynasty. Around 1300 B.C., God broke through to a man named Moses, born a Hebrew but raised Egyptian in the Pharaoh's own palace. Moses became the great leader of the Hebrews, leading them from slavery to the Promised Land. But first, Pharaoh had to be persuaded that releasing a half million brick-making Israelites was a politically correct move.

Moses used a variety of persuasive tactics. This one struck at Egypt's most precious natural resource—water. To demonstrate God's determination that Pharaoh free the Hebrew slaves, Moses changed the

Nile River from water to blood, effectively closing the world's greatest waterway to all barges, ships, and bathers—not to mention an entire Egyptian nation that needed drinking water. How did Moses do it?

Blood is composed of a complex combination of plasma, platelets, red and white cells, hormones, protein, carbohydrates, and fats, so let's rule out Moses' sprinkling a trickle of blood into the river and changing its entire chemistry. Let's also rule out the red dye some grocers use to make roadkill look like T-bone steak. A person could ponder a long time about the bag of tricks up Moses' sleeve—unless there were no tricks. We could take Moses' declaration at face value: God himself had determined to rescue his people, and every element of nature was marshaled to serve this end. No wonder the mystery of the Nile is a wonder that chemistry textbooks cannot explain!

To learn more about the Nile's red-letter day, read Exodus 7.

CuRiOuS CoNNEcTiOnS

STICKS, RODS, AND SHEPHERDS' STAFFS
The Bible relates many strange stories about common, ordinary objects like sticks, wooden rods, and shepherds' staffs that do uncommon and extraordinary things.

THE STICK THAT MADE AN AX HEAD FLOAT
The prophet Elisha stood on the banks of the Jordan River, helping students cut down trees to build a new dormitory. As they worked, one student's borrowed ax head fell off the handle and sank into the water. It was made of iron, a rare metal in those days, and quite valuable. Frantic, the student asked Elisha to help him. Elisha inquired where the ax head had fallen, and the anxious student showed him the spot. Elisha cut a stick and threw it into the river. Miraculously, the ax head defied gravity and the rushing current and floated to the surface, where the man was able to retrieve it. (See 2 Kings 6:1-7.)

A WOODEN ROD THAT BUDDED
Moses told each of the 12 tribal chiefs of Israel to bring a wooden rod with his name written on it to be placed in the inner room of the

Tabernacle. The man whose rod was chosen by God would have authority to rule over Israel under Moses. They would know the man of God's choice because buds would grow on his rod. So each man, including Aaron, brought a rod with his name on it, and Moses put the rods in the Tabernacle. The next morning, Moses and the tribal chiefs knew that God's choice was Aaron, because Aaron's rod had budded and was blossoming, and ripe almonds were hanging from it! (See Numbers 17:1-11.)

THE SERPENT STAFF
God had chosen Moses to return to Egypt and lead God's people out of slavery. But Moses was unsure and hesitant and gave many excuses why he couldn't do it. God told Moses to throw his shepherd's staff on the ground. He did, and it became a snake. When he picked it up by the tail, it became a shepherd's staff again. Moses used that staff to perform many signs that convinced (albeit temporarily) the king of Egypt to let God's people go. (See Exodus 4:1-5.)

STICKS AND STONES
Moses and the people of Israel had escaped from Egyptian slavery but faced a new challenge of a hostile wilderness. When they reached a desert place that had no water, the thirsty people began complaining and grumbling against Moses. God told Moses to strike a rock with his shepherd's staff. When Moses obeyed, water came gushing out, enough for all the people and their animals. Years later, the Israelites came to another desert place where there was no water. This time, God told Moses to speak to a rock, and he would find water. But instead of speaking to the rock, Moses struck it twice with his staff, and water came out. Because he had not followed God's instructions, Moses was not allowed to enter the Promised Land with the people. (See Exodus 17:1-6; Numbers 20:1-12.)

DID YOU KNOW?

Who survived 40 days without food or water?
Fasting has enjoyed a revival in popularity for its health and spiritual benefits. Yet prolonged fasts are unusual. A courageous

dieter might try to abstain from food for a week. But how does 40 days without food—or even water—sound? Doctors would call such behavior suicidal. We learn that Moses did just that— abstaining from all nourishment for 40 days (Exodus 34:28). A person can survive without eating any food for 28 days. But water is even more crucial to life. A person can go without water for only seven days. How did Moses survive without water for 40 days? Perhaps angels ministered to his needs, as they did when Christ undertook a similar fast in the desert (Mark 1:13). Perhaps he was sustained by God himself as he waited on Mount Sinai.

STRANGE BUT TRUE

Elijah, World-Class Sprinter

How did a prophet outrun a team of horses?

His name connotes the image of a grizzled, tough-minded, sandpaper-voiced giant who tolerates no compromise with the truth. Indeed, of all the ancient prophets, Elijah faced the hardest challenges and addressed the most recalcitrant political leaders. One of those leaders was Ahab, supported and abetted (some might say controlled) by his cunning wife, Jezebel.

At a showdown at Mt. Carmel, Elijah challenged 450 pagan priests, Ahab's religious army, to call down fire on the carcass of a slain bull. The priests chanted, prayed, danced, and literally whipped themselves into a frenzy, but understandably, no cosmic fire appeared. Then Elijah prayed, but to make the occasion even more dramatic, he first doused the carcass with water. God answered the faithful prophet's prayer, and fire shot from heaven, consuming the carcass and the wet altar it rested on. None of the priests survived the incident either.

Distressed beyond words, Ahab raced to his chariot and sped toward Jezreel, 17 miles away. Not only were his priests gone, but a huge rainstorm was about to end the drought of the century and, of more immediate concern, bog down the wheels of his carriage in the same kind of mud that stopped Hitler's army in Russia. Everyone was speeding home, in fact, except Elijah, who was left without a ride.

But wait. From his chariot Ahab could see the prophet on foot up ahead. Running. Racing. Striding. Galloping. What's this! Elijah would arrive at Jezreel before Ahab's speeding horses, and Jezebel would hear the bad news from him!

How can a man run faster than horses over a distance of 17 miles after a hot day's work outside?

Athletic feats of strength and endurance always provoke our awe and wonder, for sometimes, it seems, mere people can outperform even our grandest human expectations. The limitations we place on human performance are broken, to our amazement. For years we wondered if anyone would ever run the mile in four minutes. Now we wonder if anyone will break the time of 3:30:00.

The force which powered Elijah that day came from the same energy source that ignited the burning altar—the power of God. In both cases, these miraculous things should not have happened. In both cases, they did.

Elijah's run is described in 1 Kings 18.

CURIOUS CONNECTIONS

MEMORABLE MEALS

In ancient times, meals were occasions of great importance. Business would be conducted over meals, and great feasts would celebrate ancient treaties. Many of these ancient feasts provided an occasion of great joy to those who attended. But other celebrants faced fates far worse than indigestion.

THE MOST EXPENSIVE MEAL IN THE BIBLE

Esau and Jacob, twin sons born to Isaac and Rebekah, had little in common. Esau, the older boy, liked the outdoors and won a reputation as a fine hunter. Jacob was more settled, preferring to stay at home. One day Esau came home hungry while Jacob was cooking a stew. Esau demanded some, but Jacob insisted that he would give it to him only if the elder brother agreed to sell his rights as the firstborn son.

Esau agreed without thinking, thus giving up all the wealth and power due him according to the custom of his day. That one expensive meal would eventually change the course of Middle Eastern history. Jacob's descendants became the people of Israel, while Esau's became the nation of Edom, which eventually vanished. (See Genesis 25:27-34.)

A COSMIC CATERER?

The wedding host had committed a significant *faux pas*—he had run out of wine. Even inferior wine would have placated his guests at that point, but there was none to be found. Jesus, an invited guest, sized up the situation (at his mother's request) and ordered six large, stone water jugs be filled to the top with water. Then the servants dipped a sample and gave it to the host, who tasted it. Not only had the water turned into wine, but it surpassed anything that had been served at the ceremony (John 2:3-11). Scholars often date the beginning of Jesus' ministry with this wedding miracle at Cana.

OFF WITH HIS HEAD

Prophets can be annoying at times—especially when their condemnations are directed at you personally. Herod Antipas, a ruler over Galilee and Perea, felt this way about John the Baptist, who pointed out to all who would listen how Herod had taken for himself his brother's wife, Herodias. Because of this, Herod had the prophet locked up. But one night, on Herod's birthday, the daughter of Herodias danced for him and his dinner guests and pleased him so much that he promised to give her whatever she asked for. Prompted by her mother, she asked for the head of John the Baptist on a platter, which is what she got. (See Matthew 14:1-12; Mark 6:14-29.)

MASTERS OF DISGUISE

The following people tried to cloak their identities from other people. In some cases, they had good cause for doing so. But others had selfish reasons for hiding themselves and paid dearly for their deception.

Name	Disguise / Reason / Reference
Adam and Eve	Fig leaves sewn together / To hide their sin from God *Genesis 3:7*
Jacob	Goat skins / To deceive his father, Isaac, so he would receive Esau's blessing *Genesis 27:16*
Tamar	Veil / To protest Judah's broken promise that he would give his son to her in marriage *Genesis 38:14*
Michal	Goat skins and stone idol / To deceive Saul into thinking David was ill while he made his escape *1 Samuel 19:13*
Saul	Common clothing / Since mediums had been forbidden in Israel, Saul wore a disguise to consult with a spiritualist. *1 Samuel 28:8*
Jeroboam's wife	Clothing / Not wishing to be known as the wife of Israel's wicked king, she disguised herself to consult with the prophet Ahijah. *1 Kings 14:2*
Unnamed prophet	Bandage / He disguised himself so he could expose the folly of King Ahab's treaty with Aram. *1 Kings 20:38*
Ahab	Clothing of a common soldier / To avoid attack from the warriors of Aram; he was killed anyway *1 Kings 22:30*
Josiah	Clothing of a common soldier / Ignoring the warning of Neco, king of Egypt, Josiah went disguised into battle and was killed. *2 Chronicles 35:22*

Hemmed In

How could a man cut off a piece of a king's garment unnoticed?

In a deserted cave somewhere in Israel's hardscrabble wastelands, David and Saul were in the same place at the same time, but only one of them knew it.

Let's set the stage for this odd encounter. As David's popularity grew after he killed Goliath, King Saul's jealousy accelerated until His Royal Highness could no longer hear David's name without flying into a rage. Saul set out with 3,000 soldiers to catch David and finish him off. Meanwhile David, now a hunted fugitive, gathered about 400 other outcasts around him.

With tensions mounting, David fled to the wilderness, and Saul pursued. One day, the hunter came close to his prey but didn't know it. To escape Saul's approaching scouts, David and his men hid in a cave. Then, as luck and physical necessity would have it, Saul rode right up to the mouth of that cave. He went inside (maybe kings weren't supposed to relieve themselves in public). While he was there, David got close enough to slice off the edging on Saul's royal robe.

But why didn't David just do away with the tyrant who was making his life so awful? Hadn't the great prophet Samuel anointed David to be Israel's next king? His men urged him to act decisively. Kill Saul and seize the throne! David refused. He had great respect for Saul's office, if not for the man himself. David believed that God had placed Saul on the throne and that to resist God's will was a serious matter.

After Saul left the cave, David felt awkward and regretful; he had shamed the king by cutting his robe. He knew he could have killed the man who wanted to kill him, but he was glad he chose to restrain himself. So while Saul was still within earshot, David called an apology from across the valley, and Saul replied with his own apology. A chance meeting seems to have been the foundation of a tentative truce.

But we still might wonder . . . how did these enemies get to the same dark cave in the middle of the En-gedi wilderness, within inches of each other? Even more puzzling: Why didn't Saul ever notice?

To learn more about this strange meeting, read 1 Samuel 24.

CURIOUS CONNECTIONS

SCRIPTURE STREAKERS

Nudity and nakedness; in the buff and in the raw—we use many different words for being in the state of undress. It is a cause for awkwardness, embarrassment, and some bright red blushing. Many Bible readers are surprised by the amount of nudity described in Scripture. Of course, the classic biblical occurrence of nudity is Adam and Eve (Genesis 2:25). But other incidents, such as Samson stripping 30 men of their clothes (Judges 14:19), are a bit more bizarre.

THE NAKED BIOGRAPHER

Only the Gospel of Mark contains a curious fact about the details of Jesus' arrest and trial. After Jesus was seized and led away, some of the soldiers evidently noticed a young man "clothed only in a linen nightshirt" following Jesus. They grabbed him, but he managed to wriggle away. In the struggle, he lost his garment and fled naked. How did Mark know about this streaker? Perhaps because he was that naked young man! Many scholars believe that this odd incident was Mark's way of placing himself in the drama, as if to say *I was there also.* (See Mark 14:51-52.)

EXPOSED EMISSARIES

Typically, ambassadors to other countries are treated with respect and honor. When King David sent a delegation to the Ammonites to express sympathy over their king's death, he expected his party to be treated respectfully. Instead, Hanun, the new king, ordered them to be shaved and their clothing sheared off at the waist (2 Samuel 10:4). In ancient times, prisoners of war were denigrated in this fashion, but this wasn't acceptable protocol for entertaining dignified delegates. Such humiliation angered King David greatly; he considered it an act of war. Over 40,000 Ammonite soldiers perished in the war that resulted from this incident.

SEVEN SHAMED SONS OF SCEVA

Exorcising demons isn't a game. The seven sons of a Jewish priest named Sceva learned that lesson one fateful day (Acts 19:13-16). They were attempting to exorcise an evil spirit by invoking Jesus' name, although they really had no expressed belief in the Christian faith. They were not prepared for the challenge that greeted them, however. Instead of obediently leaving the possessed individual, the evil spirit cried out, "I know Jesus, and I know Paul. But who are you?" The demon proceeded to savagely attack the faithless sons of Sceva, leaving them stripped naked and bleeding.

STRANGE BUT TRUE

Gideon's Army

Three hundred men overwhelm a huge Midianite force

Their soldiers as numerous as the sands of the sea, the Midianites never expected the terrible onslaught that was coming. The sun set and the land grew dark. Suddenly, in the pitch black of the hill area surrounding their valley, 1,000 lights appeared—as if floating fire had been sent down from the heavens in a perfect halo. Then, as the Midianites stared in increasing mystification, trumpets blasted with a ferocity that shook the ground!

The Midianites heard the mighty roar of a unified cry: "A sword for the Lord and for Gideon!" It seemed like the sound of a million warriors. Convinced that they were surrounded, the Midianites began to flee in fear and panic. As their confusion manifested itself, they turned on each other with swords and destroyed each other with their own hands.

For this battle Gideon had started out with 32,000 men. However, the God of Israel wanted the Israelites to depend on him for victory, not on their own strength. Most were dismissed because they trembled with fear. The remaining 10,000 were tested by the way they drank water! All the men who kneeled down to drink were dismissed. But the few who lapped the water from their hands portrayed instinctive warrior qualities—readiness for any possible attack, eyes up, and on their feet.

It was these Israelites who watched in fascination as the enemy self-destructed in the valley below. Their God, the God of Israel, had given them victory that day through Gideon. Contrary to what the people in the valley thought, only 300 Hebrew soldiers had stood on the hills. Gideon gave them each a trumpet and an empty jar with a torch inside. He then split his men into three sections. At his command, the soldiers blew their trumpets, broke their jars, held their torches above their heads, and with a mighty roar cried out, "A sword for the Lord and for Gideon!" Gideon's masterful planning startled and terrified the Midianites and won a great victory for his people.

Read Judges 6–7 for a complete wrap-up of the victory.

CURIOUS CONNECTIONS

BRUSHES WITH DEATH
The Bible is filled with stories of people who barely escape with their lives—some because they were in the wrong place at the wrong time, others because of what they believed.

CALL ME ISHMAEL
The elderly Sarah finally became pregnant and bore a son for her husband, Abraham. Abraham, however, according to the custom of his day, had already fathered a child by Sarah's maidservant, Hagar. Having borne a proper heir, Sarah wanted Hagar and Hagar's son, Ishmael, sent away. The two wandered in the desert until their water ran out. Hagar wept because she knew her son would soon die. But God heard the boy's cries and revealed to Hagar a well, which saved their lives. Ishmael grew up to be the father of a great nation. (See Genesis 21:9-21.)

ROOM SERVICE
A prophet never won popularity contests. He or she usually delivered God's words at the risk of rejection and confrontation. Elijah,

for instance, always found himself at odds with Israel's wicked king Ahab. Once, after warning Ahab of an upcoming drought, God sent Elijah off to hide in a cave. But God did not let his prophet die there. He sent ravens with food to feed Elijah until the time was right for his return. (See 1 Kings 17:1-9.)

GENOCIDE
A defeated people is often a hated people. Haman, trusted minister to King Xerxes of Persia, hated the enslaved Jewish people so much that he convinced the king to sentence them to death. What the king and Haman did not realize, however, was that Esther, King Xerxes' favorite wife, was a Jew. Before the deadly action could be carried out, Esther interceded before the king for her people, thus risking her own life. The king not only stopped the scheduled slaughter, but he had the treacherous Haman put to death. (See the book of Esther.)

SHIPWRECKED AND SNAKEBIT
Probably few people in the Bible cheated death as much as the apostle Paul. During his lifetime he was beaten with whips and rods, stoned, and robbed. In one series of events in the book of Acts, his nephew learned of a plot to kill him, so Paul had to be rushed away. Later on board a ship to Rome, a great storm hit, forcing the ship aground and nearly drowning the entire crew. They landed on the island of Malta, where a poisonous snake bit Paul's hand. But much to everyone's amazement, he shook off the snake and walked away unharmed. God had promised to send Paul to Rome; not even a deadly viper could stop those plans! Church tradition maintains that Paul in fact died in Rome later, beheaded by the emperor. (See Acts 23:12-35; 27:1-28:6.)

DID YOU KNOW?

Why were Jesus' healings of lepers so remarkable?
Lepers were feared and widely shunned in ancient Israel. An incurable and disfiguring malady, leprosy caused inflammatory skin ulcers that often became infected and sometimes killed their vic-

tims. The only treatment for lepers was a strict quarantine. Few God-fearing Jews would have anything to do with lepers. Not only was the disease contagious, but anyone who touched a leper was considered ceremonially unclean and not allowed to participate in worship or have social contact for an extended time. But Jesus refused to heed the common taboos and healed many lepers. Nor did he ever contract the dreaded disease. Jesus' amazing work brought both physical and spiritual relief to a group languishing in neglect and hatred.

STRANGE BUT TRUE

The Dreamer

A man's unique supernatural gift propels him to power

Perhaps no other account in all of Scripture illustrates the strange vicissitudes of life more vividly than the biography of Joseph. Joseph was born into privilege. He was the eleventh—and favorite—son of Jacob, one of the patriarchs of Israelite history. Though Joseph was loved by his father, he was hated by his brothers because of his favored status. Joseph stoked his brothers' hatred by telling them of dreams he had—dreams in which his brothers bowed down to him.

One day the brothers could contain their rage no longer. They seized Joseph and threw him into a pit. Their first thought was to kill him, but they changed their minds when they saw a caravan heading for Egypt. Instead of murdering Joseph, his brothers sold him as a slave to members of the caravan. They returned home and told their father that Joseph had been killed by a wild beast.

In Egypt, Joseph became the trusted servant of Potiphar, an official in the king's court. Unfortunately, Potiphar's trust was shattered by one false accusation against Joseph. Without so much as a court hearing, Joseph was thrown into prison. He was doomed, or so he thought. But a perplexing turn of events raised him to unexpected heights.

In prison, Joseph met the king's cup-bearer and the king's baker.

Both men were troubled by strange and mysterious dreams. When they told Joseph their dreams, Joseph interpreted the strange visions for them. Days later his words came to pass in precisely the way he had announced. What kind of special powers did Joseph possess? How could he interpret these dreams? Joseph merely attributed his ability to the God of Israel, a God not worshiped in Egypt.

Two years later, Pharaoh had a dream. His advisors could not even begin to interpret it. Joseph was summoned from the prison to decipher the strange, troubling images. After a moment of silence, Joseph declared the visions meant that Egypt would be blessed with seven years of abundance, followed by seven years of famine. In grateful response, Pharaoh appointed Joseph second-in-command. Again, Joseph downplayed his own abilities and spoke instead of the power of God. And just as he predicted, the seven years of abundance came, as did the seven years of famine.

In Bible times, God often used dreams to communicate plans and ideas important to his purpose to particular people. We must keep in mind that without books and the conveniences of modern telecommunications, the supernatural vision may have been the "preferred" way of conveying truths to God's followers. But does God still communicate this way today? Many would say he does.

Joseph's appointment to second-in-command remains an astonishing moment in ancient history. How do we explain his rise from an impoverished foreigner to an imperial leader? Joseph himself would explain it to his brothers later as part of a divine plan. "God turned into good what you meant for evil. He brought me to the high position I have today so I could save the lives of many people" (Genesis 50:20). And that is the best explanation of all.

For more on Joseph's story, see Genesis 37–50.

CURIOUS CONNECTIONS

THE RACE FOR CHILDREN

The practice of taking more than one wife was common in many Middle Eastern cultures, but it often caused great strife in the families affected. To secure their husband's favor, wives would try to produce children—a sign of fertility and of God's blessing. The struggle for heirs often encouraged wives to compete with other wives and concubines to secure affection. Here are some of the more famous "children races" found in Scripture.

SARAH AND HAGAR

Sarah, wife of the patriarch Abraham, could not bear children. As was the custom of the day, she gave her Egyptian servant, Hagar, to Abraham so he could produce an heir. Hagar became pregnant, but the tension between Sarah and Hagar was so keen that Hagar ran away. She eventually went back to her mistress and gave birth to a son, Ishmael. But after Sarah unexpectedly became pregnant and gave birth to Isaac, she wanted her "competition," so to speak, out of the picture, so she ordered Abraham to send Hagar and Ishmael away. With regret Abraham did so, but he had God's assurance that the two would be taken care of. Ishmael grew up to be an expert archer and the father of the Ishmaelites, a nomadic people of the Middle East. (See Genesis 17; 21.)

RACHEL AND LEAH

No contest between competing wives was as fierce or enduring as the rivalry between the sisters Rachel and Leah. Daughters of Laban, they both wed Jacob, though the circumstances of their marriages had created a rift that would never heal. Jacob had not intended to marry Leah, but Laban had tricked him into doing so. Jacob was allowed to marry Rachel seven years later, and the sisters tried to prove their favor before God and Jacob by bearing children. Leah bore Jacob six sons and a daughter, but Rachel was barren for a long time. Eventually, however, she gave birth to Joseph and Benjamin. The wives' maids, Bilhah and Zilpah, also produced sons for Jacob. Altogether Jacob had 12 sons—the founders of the 12 tribes of Israel. (See Genesis 29:16-35.)

HANNAH AND PENINNAH

Hannah was desperate to have children. Her husband, Elkanah, dearly loved her, but his other wife, Peninnah, taunted her because of her childlessness. So Hannah prayed earnestly for a son, telling God that she would dedicate him to holy service if her request was granted. God heard those prayers, and Hannah bore a son named Samuel. After the boy was weaned, Hannah fulfilled her vow and took young Samuel to the Tabernacle. He grew up assisting Eli, Israel's chief priest, and became a great prophet who anointed Israel's first two kings, Saul and David. (See 1 Samuel 1.)

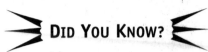

DID YOU KNOW?

Who initiated mass divorce among the exiles returning from Babylon?

The laws of Moses clearly declared that the people of Israel were to keep themselves separate from pagan nations. Yet over time this regulation was ignored as men took wives from neighboring lands. The prophet Ezra was among those returning from Babylon. When he heard about the widespread intermarriage that had taken place, he called for a prolonged period of self-examination and repentance. Later he proposed that the exiles divorce their pagan wives to turn away God's anger. His advice was heeded, and hundreds of men sent their wives away. (See Ezra 9:1–10:44.)

STRANGE BUT TRUE

Rushing Wind

Visitors to Jerusalem get an unexpected encounter with a new religious phenomenon

The sound of the wind had been like nothing they'd ever heard before. The confidence of the leader was also unusual. Yet the language—no, make that the languages—being spoken could not have been more familiar.

The scene was Jerusalem, several weeks after the death and resurrection of the one called Jesus, the Christ. It was the day of Pentecost, 50 days after the Jewish Passover. Jews from many countries were in the city. A small group of men who had followed Jesus the closest were in the city as well. About 120 counted themselves as believers at that time, and they were led by the 12 disciples.

Gathered together in a house, the twelve heard and felt a violent wind. Amazingly, tongues of fire then seemed to land on their heads. Neighbors and passersby came running. A crowd gathered, including scores of visitors gathered for the festival. The disciples were all talking at once, using the languages of the foreign visitors. How could these Galileans—mostly uneducated fishermen—be speaking in the languages of Mesopotamia, of Judea and Cappadocia, of Egypt and Libya, of Asia and beyond?

They were not babbling but describing the work of God through Jesus whom they worshiped. "They must be drunk!" some jeered. But Peter—the same man who had turned his back on Jesus during his trial and crucifixion—raised his voice and gave his explanation. He matched up what was happening with an Old Testament prophecy that the wind and fire signified the coming of God's Spirit. The time had come, Peter declared, for all the world to know about God's redemption.

The wind, the fire, and the languages were indeed mystifying. Yet this display of God's power got the attention of about 3,000 people who joined the tiny movement that day. Pentecost is often called the birthday of the church that now claims over a billion members.

For the complete story, check out Acts 2.

CuRiOuS CoNNEcTiOnS

CIRCUMSTANTIAL CIRCUMCISION
The ancients practiced circumcision of male boys, just as many people do today. For the Israelites, this practice identified them with God and his people. It was an initiation rite. But sometimes the deed was carried out in threatening or bizarre circumstances.

THE FORGOTTEN DEED
Moses should have remembered. He had been entrusted with leading Israel out of bondage and bringing renewal to God's people. Yet he had neglected to circumcise his own son—a major blunder for the

new leader of God's people! So God confronted Moses and was about to kill him when Zipporah, Moses' wife, grabbed a flint knife and circumcised the boy, then chastised Moses for his obtuse behavior. (See Exodus 4:24-26.)

THE PRICE FOR A BRIDE
As a result of David's victory over the giant Goliath, David was entitled to marry the daughter of King Saul. Yet Saul, who was jealous of David, demanded a rather unusual dowry for his daughter. The king ordered David to bring him the foreskins of 100 Philistines. Saul secretly hoped that David would be killed by the Philistines while collecting the dowry. The king was unpleasantly surprised when David returned later with 200 Philistine foreskins—twice the dowry Saul had asked for. Since it's unlikely that the Philistines willingly parted with this particular part of their bodies, we can assume that David killed the Philistines before performing the circumcisions. (See 1 Samuel 18:17-30.)

A SOURCE OF CONTROVERSY
Timothy, the son of a Jewish mother and a Greek father, was an early convert to Christianity. This young man was so highly thought of in Lystra and Iconium that Paul decided to take Timothy with him on a missionary journey. Paul knew that he and Timothy would encounter Jewish converts on their journey. He also knew that these Jewish converts would be offended by an uncircumcised son of a Jewish mother. In order to avoid this potential problem, Paul circumcised Timothy before the journey. (See Acts 16:1-4.)

STRANGE BUT TRUE

The Venom of the Viper

A bronze serpent produces miraculous healings

Snakes are thinner and shorter than people and not nearly as intelligent, but we fear them much more than they fear us. Figure that out! Face-to-face with a snake, people give way. Even the all-daring Indiana Jones once admitted, "I hate snakes!"

In the Bible, a serpent led the first humans into big trouble. But in a surprising turnaround during their wilderness years, the Israelites were saved from a deadly invasion of poisonous snakes by a serpent made from bronze. A symbol of what the people feared most became their deliverance from the venom of the viper. How could a serpent made of metal diffuse toxic chemicals already inside a snakebite victim's bloodstream?

Some of the Bible's mysteries might be explained by laws of nature, but this one seems to defy them all. Lethal chemicals circulating through a person's body seem unlikely to be altered by visual sightings of any kind. But perhaps we're not really *seeing* the issue here. Can even the most tough-minded scientist doubt that a powerful and largely unexplained connection exists between the mind and the body? Cancer patients are told that laughter, joy, and merriment are related to longer survival rates. The effects of neurological diseases are sometimes oddly postponed by positive mental attitudes. We don't know how or why, but something is going on behind the scenes that connects what we believe with how our body actually responds to the microscopic vermin inside us.

In this case, it seems clear that a "little extra" antidote helped the bodies of those who obeyed Moses and looked at the bronze serpent, for all who looked lived. Sadly, we know that many positive-attitude patients still succumb to their illnesses. A positive attitude brings only a statistical improvement, whereas each Israelite experienced direct and personal healing.

The bare facts stand by themselves. We know that Moses prayed and displayed the snake (Numbers 21:7-9). The miracle of prayer and faith is the only explanation given for the recovery. We must take seriously the intention of the writer of Numbers: God had brought about a mighty miracle among his people.

For more on the Israelites' detox program, read Numbers 21:4-9.

UNDER THE INFLUENCE

Fermented beverages have contributed to people's bizarre behavior for centuries. From the first days of Bible history, humans have paid the price for imbibing too much. Here are some of the more notable episodes of public intoxication—with the tragic results.

Imbiber	Situation	Consequences	Reference
Lot	Desperate to preserve their family line, his daughters got him drunk and then slept with him to get pregnant.	The sons these women bore became the ancestors of Israel's great enemies Moab and Ammon.	Genesis 19:30-38
Nabal	He had a stroke the morning after a night of drinking and died ten days later.	His selfish living and opposition to King David sealed his fate.	1 Samuel 25:1-42
Uriah	Though drunk, he refused to go home and sleep with his wife while his men were in battle.	Dismayed by Uriah's sense of honor, David had Joab assign Uriah to the fiercest part of the battle, where Uriah was killed.	2 Samuel 11:1-27
Amnon	While drunk, he was killed by Absalom's men in retaliation for Amnon's rape of Tamar.	Amnon's careless life and heartless treatment of his sister sowed the seeds of his disaster.	2 Samuel 13:1-39
Elah	This king of Israel was assassinated while he was drunk.	His death fulfilled a prophecy spoken by Jehu.	1 Kings 16:8-12
Ben-Hadad	This king chose to get drunk even though hostilities with Israel were about to break out.	Ill-prepared for Ahab's attack, the Aramean army suffered heavy losses and fled.	1 Kings 20:1-22
Xerxes	During a drunken party, this king ordered his wife Vashti to appear before the guests.	Vashti refused and was banished from the palace, setting the stage for Esther's rise.	Esther 1:1-22
Belshazzar	While drunk, this king used vessels from the Temple in Jerusalem as wine cups.	Belshazzar's disrespect for the holy vessels of the Temple led to his downfall.	Daniel 5:1-31

ANIMAL TALES

Anyone who has toured a zoo knows that there are some strange-looking animals. Here are some strange stories involving animals that appear in the Bible.

A REAL HORNETS' NEST

A swarm of angry hornets makes for some very unpleasant company. The peoples dwelling in Canaan discovered this firsthand as the Israelites marched into their midst. The Lord had promised his people that he would send hornets ahead of them to drive the inhabitants from the Promised Land! Joshua, in his farewell address, indicates that this actually happened: "I [the Lord] sent hornets ahead of you to drive out the two kings of the Amorites" (Joshua 24:12). Other ancient records attest to similar incidents in which entire towns were forced to evacuate because of angry insects.

DON'T GET THAT BALD GUY MAD

In Israel's culture, youths were expected to show deep respect for their elders. Mosaic law, for instance, meted out severe penalties for children who failed to honor their parents. Perhaps that explains Elisha's angry reaction to a band of young men who confronted him on the road to Bethel. They began teasing and insulting him, chanting "Go away, you baldhead!" Elisha looked at them and cursed them. At that moment, two bears charged out of the woods and mauled 42 of Elisha's detractors. Thus avenged, Elisha continued on his way. (See 2 Kings 2:23-24.)

ZERO TOLERANCE FOR REPEAT OFFENDERS

Oxen with nasty tempers probably did not last too long in Israel. According to the law of Moses, an ox that killed a man or woman could be stoned to death and its owner fined. If the ox had a history of harming people and the owner did not take steps to prevent such behavior, the owner and the animal would both be killed. (See Exodus 21:28-30.)

STRANGE BUT TRUE

Samson's Amazing Strength

What was the secret of his astonishing power?

If you ever needed an escort, a bodyguard, or a friend to walk with you down a dark alley, Samson was the guy. Possessed of legendary strength, he fought lions barehanded, mangled unsuspecting enemies, and laid to rest a contingent of 1,000 troops, using only a donkey's jawbone. His last act of brute force was to pull down a stone temple using the power of his upper torso. Samson was not immortal; the stone that crushed a party of Philistines crushed him to death, too. But no one before or since has matched his raw strength. According to Scripture, the source of that peerless power was God himself.

Men who make a profession of bodybuilding can develop an extensive and well-defined muscle system, but still they seem to be minor leaguers compared to Samson. Certainly he had something inside that was most unusual—perhaps a rare genetic makeup combined with intense willpower and unsurpassed self-confidence. But does that explain his extraordinary feats? Consider, too, that his parents, after an amazing encounter with an angel, had dedicated Samson's life to God's service even before he was born. They raised him according to the vows of the Nazirite sect—which meant, among other things, that he could not cut his hair.

Samson's physical prowess, however, was not always put to good use. He could be vengeful and impulsive, and his choice of partners ill advised and naive. His trust in a treacherous woman, Delilah, led to his demise. Something about his uncut hair related directly to his strength; a barber was to Samson as kryptonite was to Superman. Samson could not explain it, but he knew that a haircut would strip his strength. And that's exactly what Delilah arranged. She lured him to his enemies and conspired to have him bound and blinded. He remained a prisoner until he ended his life—and the lives of hundreds of Philistines—by destroying the temple of Dagon with his own hands.

So the mystery remains. How can one man possess such over-whelming strength? And what's the connection between the protein of a person's hair and the power of his deltoids? In the end, we may conclude with the author of Judges that God gave Samson such incredible strength to use in his service.

To find out more about Samson's adventurous life, read Judges 13–16.

◼ THE FASCINATING MIRACLES OF JESUS

All miracles are astounding. But the miracles Jesus performed were not supernatural sideshows. They were intended to confirm God's faithfulness among his people. Moreover, those who were healed or delivered from oppression often had to first display faith. It is telling that Jesus often could not perform miracles among disbelieving audiences. The miracles recorded in the Gospels are summarized below.

1. Jesus turned water to wine, symbolizing the beginning of his ministry (John 2:1-11).
2. He cured an official's sick son in Capernaum (John 4:46-54).
3. He healed Peter's mother-in-law of her fever (Luke 4:38-39).
4. He directed Peter, James, and John to an enormous amount of fish (Luke 5:1-11).
5. He healed a leper in Galilee (Matthew 8:2-4).
6. He caused a paralyzed man to walk (Mark 2:1-12).
7. He healed an invalid at the Pool of Bethesda (John 5:1-15).
8. He restored a man with a withered hand in Galilee (Matthew 12:9-13).
9. He healed a Roman officer's sick servant in Capernaum (Luke 7:1-10).
10. He raised a widow's only son from the dead in Nain (Luke 7:11-17).
11. He cast a spirit out of a blind and mute man in Galilee (Matthew 12:22-32).

12. He calmed a storm on the Sea of Galilee (Mark 4:35-41).
13. He cast a demon out of a man in the region of the Gerasenes (Luke 8:26-39).
14. He healed a woman who had a blood disorder (Matthew 9:20-22).
15. He raised Jairus's daughter from the dead (Luke 8:41-56).
16. He restored sight to two blind men in Capernaum (Matthew 9:27-31).
17. He cast a spirit out of a mute man in Capernaum (Matthew 9:32-34).
18. He fed over 5,000 people with just five loaves of bread and two fish (John 6:1-14).
19. He walked on water in the Sea of Galilee (Mark 6:45-52).
20. He cast a demon out of a girl in the region of Tyre and Sidon (Matthew 15:21-28).
21. He healed a deaf person with a speech impediment (Mark 7:31-37).
22. He fed over 4,000 people with just seven loaves of bread and a few small fish (Matthew 15:29-38).
23. He healed a blind man in Bethsaida (Mark 8:22-26).
24. He cast a demon out of a boy who was having seizures (Luke 9:37-42).
25. He caused money to be found in the mouth of a fish (Matthew 17:24-27).
26. He restored sight to a blind man in Jerusalem (John 9:1-7).
27. He healed a woman who had been crippled for 18 years (Luke 13:10-17).
28. He healed a man who suffered from dropsy (Luke 14:1-6).
29. He raised Lazarus from the dead (John 11:1-44).
30. He healed ten lepers in Samaria (Luke 17:11-19).
31. He restored sight to Bartimaeus (Mark 10:46-52).
32. He cursed a fig tree and caused it to wither (Matthew 21:18-19).
33. He reattached Malchus's ear after Peter cut it off (Luke 22:49-51).
34. He caused Peter, James, and John to catch 153 large fish (John 21:1-13).

Midnight Deliverance

Was there any connection between a tumultuous earthquake and the faith of two prisoners?

Midnight. Sitting in their dark and dreary cells, the prisoners in the damp Philippian jail listened with closed eyes to the strangely comforting songs floating through the prison. The new prisoners, Paul and Silas, were singing again. The old-timers, the ones who had been languishing in prison for years, couldn't quite figure those new prisoners out: they had been severely flogged and were in the well-guarded, bare inner cell with their feet in heavy iron stocks. Yet they were singing and praying!

The music didn't wake the jailer though. He had had a rough day.

The quiet night was suddenly interrupted when the ground under the prison began to shake! At first, it seemed like a mere tremor. But then, the quake grew more violent and more fierce. The stone walls of the prison began falling in. Even the foundations of the prison were cracked and turned. The Philippians hadn't experienced a quake like this for a long time. With dust and chunks of rock flying around, the doors of the prison cells flew open. All the captives had an incredible chance to walk away from their chains.

The mighty hand of God had shaken the prison. The old-timers couldn't believe it. They had longed for such a day, to be free from this fetid dungeon. Stunned and dazed, the prisoners did not make a break for it. All they could think of was those two strange prisoners who had spent the night singing. What was all this about? Surely it was more than coincidence that an earthquake had hit the Philippian jail holding two unique prisoners, two people who spoke of an Almighty God and sang to him all night long. In fact, that is what Luke, the writer of Acts, tells his readers. God had freed Paul, Silas, and the others to demonstrate his power.

The Philippian jailer, for one, recognized the earthquake as a divine stroke. Out of fear and wonder, he asked Paul and Silas about their God and their faith, and they talked until the dawn of the next morning. The city officials acted quickly to encourage Paul and Silas to leave the city. Shaken up emotionally as well as physically, the officials decided to free these two strangers before more trouble came. Paul and Silas went on to preach their message throughout Asia and Europe, and the world was never the same again.

For more information about this bizarre earthquake, read Acts 16:16-40.

CURIOUS CONNECTIONS

FISHY STORIES

Everyone has heard about a fisherman catching what he thought was a fish only to find out it was a rubber boot. The Bible has its own fish stories, but the evidence surrounding them suggests that they are true.

FOOD FOR ALL

On two occasions, Jesus astonished his followers and detractors alike by making do with a few fish and a little bread and producing a tremendous meal. Having taught great crowds for hours, Jesus felt pity for the men, women, and children who would have to trudge many miles home to eat. Finding a few small fish and a couple loaves of bread, he ordered his disciples to pass them out to the thousands gathered. Not only did everyone eat until all were satisfied, but afterward, the disciples gathered many baskets of leftover food! (See Mark 6:30-44; 8:1-10.)

BETTER THAN A TAX REFUND

When Jesus and his disciples arrived in Capernaum, tax collectors from the Temple asked Peter if Jesus was going to pay the tax required of adult males. Peter said yes, but met with Jesus to discuss the matter. Jesus implied it was unnecessary to pay the tax, but he did not want to offend the tax collectors. He told Peter to go down to the sea and throw in a fishing line and hook. He was to open the mouth of the first fish he caught and pay the taxes with what he found inside. Peter, himself a fisherman, obeyed and went to the seashore with a fishing line. When he caught the first fish, he opened its mouth and found a coin inside, just the right amount to pay the taxes for himself and Jesus. (See Matthew 17:24-27.)

THE CATCH OF THE DAY
One day Jesus was preaching beside a lake, and a mob of people crowded around to hear him. He stepped into an empty fishing boat and asked the owner, Simon Peter, to take him out into the water so he could speak to the people. After he finished speaking, Jesus told Peter to go out into deeper water and Peter would catch a lot of fish. Peter said that he and his crew had fished all night and hadn't caught a thing. "But," he said, "if you say so, we'll try again." They rowed out to the spot where they had caught nothing all night and let down their nets. Incredibly, their nets were suddenly so full of fish they started to tear. Peter called to his partners, who rushed out in the other boat to help. Together, they hauled in so many fish both boats were about to sink. Amazed, Peter fell at Jesus' feet. Jesus told Peter, "From now on you'll be fishing for people!" When they reached shore, Peter and his partners left their boats and nets and followed Jesus. (See Luke 5:1-11.)

 FAQs (frequently asked questions)

FAMILY CUSTOMS

Why do so many people in Bible stories marry close relatives?
Most incidents of a person marrying a close relative occur in the earliest times of biblical history, when populations were relatively small. In some cases, marrying a relative was a favorable alternative to a bond with a pagan spouse. Rebekah, for instance, sent her son Jacob to her brother Laban for a wife because she was fearful of the influence of Hittite women (Genesis 27:46). Recall too that the law of the kinsman-redeemer (seen in the story of Ruth) provided that a man could marry the widow of his brother or other relation to preserve the property holdings of the family.

If monogamy was God's design for marriage, why did he allow kings like David and Solomon to practice polygamy?

The pattern of monogamy appears to have God's approval from the beginning (Genesis 2:21-24; Mark 10:6-9), but the practice of taking more than one wife occurs throughout the Old Testament. Lamech, Jacob, Esau, Elkanah, David, Solomon, Rehoboam, and Abijah, among others, had at least two wives and sometimes many more. Especially among royalty, polygamy was a symbol of wealth and power, and the tolerance of polygamy may have been a grudging concession to custom. It should be stated that multiple marriages often caused formidable problems for families. David could not control his children, whose crimes included rape, murder, and rebellion. The writer of 1 Kings claims that Solomon's wives led him into idolatry and spiritual indifference (1 Kings 11:1-8).

Why did the Israelites circumcise males?

Circumcision was a sign of God's covenant with Abraham and his descendants (Genesis 17:10-14). The ceremony was performed eight days after the child's birth. In the early church, circumcision became a hotly debated issue. Some Jewish Christians insisted that all male converts be circumcised, but another group, led by Paul among others, refused to make it a requirement. Paul's position eventually won the day.

What was the Nazirite vow?

Part of the law handed down to Moses included a voluntary pledge of dedication to God's service. Like monastic vows practiced centuries later by some Christians, the Naziritesvow promised abstinence from certain practices during the pledge. He or she could not drink wine or eat grapes, cut his or her hair, or touch a dead body (see Numbers 6). Perhaps the most famous (and unusual) Nazirite was Samson. His case was atypical because his parents made the vow on his behalf, apparently for his entire life. From hints we find in Scripture, some have suggested that Samuel, John the Baptist, and the apostle Paul also took this vow at some time in their lives.

Why weren't the Israelites supposed to marry outside their clan? Does this mean that God is opposed to interracial marriages?

The prohibition against intermarriage was primarily a spiritual safeguard, not a separation demanded for racial or ethnic purity. Because the Israelites alone had received God's revelation, they feared that intermarriage would soften resistance to behavior considered sinful. By and large, this fear proved to be well founded. Bad company corrupts character, so the saying goes, and intermarriages tended to erode the moral foundation of Israel much more frequently than they uplifted the culture of neighboring peoples. So serious was this problem during Judah's return from exile that the prophet Ezra ordered Judah's men to send their foreign wives and children away. (See Ezra 9:1–10:44.)

What is a concubine?

A concubine was in many ways a second-class citizen, a woman entitled to some but not all the privileges of marriage. A man could acquire a concubine either as a spoil of war or as a purchase; it follows that concubines were often the reserve of wealthy or privileged men. Concubines had some legal rights, but they were still considered property rather than equal partners. It is sad but not surprising to encounter stories of a master treating a concubine callously: Witness Hagar's abrupt dismissal by Abraham (Genesis 21:8-21) and the Levite's coldhearted offering of his concubine to the perverse men of Gibeah (Judges 19:25-28).

FATEFUL FORECASTS

Episodes of
Judgment and Woe

Death Times Two

A real estate transaction brings fatal consequences

A second body? The young men had barely returned from burying the first victim when they saw his wife's body on the floor. Was it a coincidence . . . or a double homicide?

Ananias and his wife, Sapphira, were members of the church in Jerusalem. The number of believers in the city had grown astronomically in the months and years following Jesus' death and resurrection. Their commitment to each other had grown just as remarkably, to the point of sharing their possessions and money. To meet the needs of the poor, church members who owned land—Ananias and Sapphira among them—sold their property and gave the proceeds to the church leaders to distribute among the poor.

The day's transaction started well. This couple sold some property and, as they had agreed, Ananias brought the money to the leaders. Proudly he handed it over to a man named Peter. Yet a few moments later Ananias fell over—dead before he hit the floor. Was it a heart attack?

Unaware of her husband's death, Sapphira came before the committee a few hours later. Unbelievably, she met her end in the same way—falling down, not in a faint but in death. The young men who had buried Ananias had the sad task of burying her, a short time later and a short distance away.

Great fear rippled through the young church. What had Peter said—or done—to each of them? But the other church leaders who had witnessed the double deaths verified that Peter was guilty of no wrongdoing.

Sapphira and Ananias, however, had had their own agenda: They had decided to secretly keep some of the profits from the real estate transaction for themselves and donate the balance, professing that it was the full amount. Who would be the wiser? When questioned by Peter, Sapphira had calmly replied that they had given the full profits to the church.

But they hadn't reckoned on the experience and insight of Peter, one of Jesus' handpicked followers who had been credited with some startling deeds (see the first few chapters of Acts). The other church leaders reported that Peter seemed to immediately sense that Ananias was lying about the money. "You have not lied to men but to God!" the apostle shouted. Ananias collapsed to the floor and died. Nearly the identical scene was played out when Sapphira entered the room a few hours later. Her lifeless body was carried out to be with her husband's.

One sudden death could be tossed off as coincidence. But two? Their inexplicable demise forces us to take seriously the conclusion reached by Luke, the author of Acts: the two had been judged by God for lying and deceit.

To read the full story, see Acts 4–5.

CURIOUS CONNECTIONS

SUDDEN DEATH
One second you're alive, the next you inexplicably drop dead. The Bible is filled with accounts of people whose lives were snuffed out in an instant. What had they done? What brought about such retribution?

FLASH IN THE PAN
Even having a famous father is not enough when you disobey God. Nadab and Abihu were the sons of Aaron, the brother of the great

prophet Moses and the first high priest of the Israelites. While making offerings in the Tabernacle, they burned incense to God in a pan in an improper manner. Seconds later, fiery flames shot down from heaven and incinerated them. This terrifying and sobering lesson was not lost on Aaron and his two remaining sons. (See Leviticus 10:1-3.)

THE TOUCH OF DEATH
Uzzah should have known better. The law of Moses had made clear that there were proper and improper ways to move the Ark of the Covenant. Instead of the Ark being carried on poles as the law required, it was moved on an oxcart. When the oxen stumbled, Uzzah tried to save the Ark from falling and reached out to steady it. His gesture, however well intended, disregarded the holiness of the object he touched. Uzzah died instantly, putting an immediate end to the festive procession. (See 2 Samuel 6:3-7.)

NO NEWS IS GOOD NEWS
Best known as the mentor of the prophet Samuel, Eli was the high priest of Israel during the time of the judges. Yet his own weakness as a father caused him to neglect the irreverent behavior of his sons, Hophni and Phinehas. A prophet approached Eli with news that his failure would forever hound his family, and that both his sons would die on the same day. Soon afterward, his sons carried the Ark of the Covenant into battle with the Philistines. Both were killed, and the Ark was captured. When Eli heard the report from the battlefield, he fell backwards from his seat and died instantly from a broken neck. (See 1 Samuel 4:12-21.)

DID YOU KNOW?

Who were the Nicolaitans?
In the book of Revelation (2:6), Jesus commended Ephesian Christians for hating the immoral deeds of the Nicolaitans. He even threatened to use the "sword of [his] mouth"—a metaphor for judgment— against this group in Pergamum (Revelation 2:16). Who were these people? No one knows exactly, but

Revelation does give us some clues. Christ likened the Nicolaitans to the pagan prophet Balaam, who in Moses' time had been hired by an enemy king to curse the Israelites. Later Balaam encouraged Moabite women to seduce the men of Israel. Today most scholars concur that the Nicolaitans, whoever they were, likely encouraged sexual immorality and idolatry among the early Christians. According to Revelation, this group would experience the full wrath of God.

C u R i O u S   C o N n E c T i O n S

WHAT A WAY TO GO

Though some people might argue that there is no "good" way to die, everyone would probably agree that the following deaths recorded in the Bible are particularly distasteful.

A HAIR-RAISING DEMISE

Absalom might have been known in Bible lore only for his remarkable hair. Weighing five pounds, it was so thick and heavy that he cut it but once a year. Yet Absalom, the son of King David, was vain and ambitious. He led a rebellion against his father that ended in failure. As he was riding a mule, fleeing from David's men, Absalom's hair became entangled in the branches of an oak tree. As he twisted in the air, Joab, David's general, killed him and buried his body in a forest. Absalom's death grieved David greatly, despite his son's treachery. (See 2 Samuel 18.)

DOWRY OF DEATH

Shechem, a prince, was used to getting what he wanted. When he saw Dinah, the only daughter of Jacob, he was enchanted with her beauty. He seized and raped her. Shechem, however, wanted to marry Dinah anyway, so he asked her brothers and father for permission. He promised to pay any dowry they demanded as the price for his bride. Dinah's brothers, furious with what had happened, deceived Shechem by appearing to approve of the request, provided that the men of Shechem's village undergo circumcision. While the men were recovering from their wounds, two of the brothers entered the town and killed every man there, including Shechem. Their retaliation infuriated Jacob, who feared that his neighbors would avenge the massacre. (See Genesis 34:1-31.)

A SPLITTING HEADACHE

Sisera thought he had found refuge. The commander of the Canaanite forces, he had fled on foot after losing his entire army to the Israelites. He found the tent of Heber, a member of the Kenite tribe. Because Heber's clan was on friendly terms with the Canaanite king, Sisera accepted the hospitality of Heber's wife, Jael, who led him into her tent. He fell asleep from exhaustion. Jael then crept to his side and, taking a hammer, drove a tent peg through his skull. Deborah, the prophetess and judge, would commemorate Sisera's unseemly death in song. (See Judges 4:12-24; 5:24-31.)

STRANGE BUT TRUE

The Prophet's Mistake

Lies and a lion spell doom for a man of God

The evening was eerily quiet. The setting sun cast unusual shadows on the path to Bethel. The villager wondered about the silence as she rounded the corner, then stopped dead in her tracks. An intense chill passed through her body. Directly in front of the villager was one of the biggest lions she had ever seen! More horrifying still, the lion was standing over a dead man, side by side with a donkey. The lion had neither devoured the donkey nor mauled the man! Carried away by fear, the villager ran as fast as she could back to town. Her cries were heard throughout Bethel as she recited the details of this bizarre event.

Nearby, an old prophet looked uneasily at his sons and asked them to saddle up his donkey. He was pretty sure he knew this dead stranger—a man of God who had eaten dinner at the old prophet's home that very day. The old prophet went to the spot the villager had told about and saw the lion, the donkey, and the corpse. What had happened?

Earlier that morning, the victim had entered the temple in Bethel.

All eyes were on the great King Jeroboam who was about to make a sacrifice to two golden calves—a profane sacrifice, since it was offered on the God of Israel's altar. Startling everyone around, the man of God cried out, condemning Jeroboam for his evil ways, "This is the sign of the Lord: the altar will be split apart, and the ashes on it will be poured out!" Eyes blazing in self-righteous anger, Jeroboam roared, "Seize him!" But as he stretched his hand toward the man, it shriveled up, fingers curved grotesquely inward so he could not pull it back. At that moment, the altar split apart and the ashes poured out. Relenting his anger, Jeroboam asked the man of God to intervene so that God would restore his hand; his hand became normal. Visibly relieved, Jeroboam beckoned the prophet to dine with him. But the man of God refused. He said, "Even if you were to give me half of your possessions, I would not go with you nor would I eat bread or drink water here. For I was commanded by the word of the Lord not to eat or drink or return by the way I came." And so he took another road home.

The sons of the old prophet had been present at the Temple that day. They ran home and told their father about the amazing feats of this man of God and what he had said to the king. The old prophet, perhaps skeptical of the younger man's integrity, saddled up his donkey and rode off to find him. He found the man of God resting under a tree, exhausted from lack of food and water. The old prophet said, "Come home with me and eat!" But the man of God refused, repeating what he had told the king. So the old prophet replied, "I too am a prophet." And then he lied. "An angel of the Lord told me to bring you back to my house so that you may eat and drink." Convinced, the man of God went with him.

While they were sitting at the table, a message from the Lord came to the old prophet, and he cried out, "You have defied the word of the Lord and have not kept his command. You came back and ate bread and drank water in the place where he told you not to eat or drink! Therefore, you will not be buried in the tomb of your fathers."

Soon after the man of God departed, a lion sprang on him on the road and killed him. But why? One explanation may be that he did not take seriously the warning he had received and was too easily convinced of the old prophet's story. His lack of discernment became his downfall.

The old prophet later took the man of God's lifeless body and placed it in his own tomb. Showing his affection for the fallen prophet, he told his sons that at his death he wanted to be buried next to the man of God.

For more details of this puzzling death, read 1 Kings 13.

C u R i O u S   C o N n E c T i O n S

TEMPLES OF DOOM

A house of worship, a sanctuary of quiet, a monument of beauty—such are the images we associate with a temple. But several episodes in the Bible remind us that conflict, strife, and violence can enter even those holy places.

PILLAR OF THE COMMUNITY

Samson was feared for his great strength. His mortal enemies, the Philistines, eventually discovered that his hair was the source of his power. With the help of a deceptive mistress, they cut off his hair, then bound, blinded, and enslaved him. Over time, however, Samson's hair grew back, and with it, his strength. At a great celebration in the temple of the Philistine god, Dagon, Samson was paraded before a jeering audience. Yet he got his revenge when he pushed on the supporting columns of the great building, collapsing the structure and killing thousands of his enemies as well as himself. (See Judges 16:4-30.)

A SUBTLE HINT

The Philistines rejoiced when they captured the Ark of the Covenant. An ornate container overlaid with gold, the Ark housed sacred items belonging to the Israelites. The celebration turned to horror, however, once they placed the Ark in the temple of their god, Dagon. The book of 1 Samuel records that the next morning the Philistines discovered the statue of their god facedown on the floor in front of the sacred chest. They uprighted it, but the following morning they found it facedown again, its head and hands broken off and lying on the floor in the doorway. The Philistines were also afflicted with sores and tumors, and in a panic they sent the Ark back to Israel on a oxcart. (See 1 Samuel 5:1-12.)

HORNS OF A DILEMMA
Holy places could become islands of refuge for those escaping persecution. Yet they did not guarantee safety for those guilty of crime. Abinadab and Joab had fled from King Solomon for their acts of treason; both entered the Tabernacle and grabbed the horns of the altar so they would not be killed. Abinadab was allowed to live but died shortly thereafter for another act of disloyalty. Joab did not receive even a reprieve; he was struck down beside the altar after he refused to leave the Tabernacle. (See 2 Kings 2.)

TRUST ME
Jehu, an ancient king of Israel, had little use for the priests who worshiped the pagan god Baal, but he didn't let them know that. In fact, he told them that he was their biggest supporter and wanted to personally offer a sacrifice in their temple. After he lured them and their followers there, he had them killed and the temple destroyed, turning it into a public toilet, thus ending for a time the worship of Baal in Israel. (See 2 Kings 10:19-28.)

CURIOUS CONNECTIONS

STONED
The practice of stoning a person to death has largely disappeared today. Yet in many ancient cultures, stoning was demanded for crimes against God and society. The Bible first mentions this practice in Exodus 8:26, where Moses voices the fear that Hebrew worship would incite the Egyptians to stone God's people. The Books of the Law mandated death by stoning as punishment for human sacrifice, blasphemy, sorcery, and other crimes. Yet innocent people too became victims, as the record of Scripture shows.

THE FIRST EXECUTION
The first record of a stoning occurs in Leviticus 24:23. Here we read that the unnamed son of an Israelite woman and Egyptian man was

put to death for cursing the name of the Lord. It is interesting to note that the stoning occurs after the law is given; Exodus 20:7 declares that the "Lord will not let you go unpunished if you misuse his name." Hence the man would have had fair warning that his crime would have been punishable by death. Later, another Israelite was stoned for gathering wood on the Sabbath. (See Numbers 15:32-35.)

COLLECTIVE GUILT

A beautiful robe imported from Babylon, hundreds of silver coins, a bar of gold—the young Israelite named Achan saw the rich plunder that had been seized from the Canaanites. Rather than destroy the loot as God had ordered, Achan decided to keep a portion for himself, burying it under his tent. But after a disastrous battle and an episode of soul-searching, Joshua was able to discern that Israel's misfortune had been caused by Achan's disobedience. Immediately Achan and his family, his possessions, and the hidden plunder were taken to the valley of Achor. The community stoned Achan and his family to death and buried everything under a great pile of rocks. (See Joshua 7:1-26.)

GREED KILLS

King Ahab thought he had offered a fair deal to Naboth. In exchange for Naboth's vineyard, which was situated near his palace, Ahab offered a handsome price or the promise of better land. Naboth refused the offer, however. Jezebel, Ahab's wife, then cooked up a wicked scheme to seize the land. She coerced the elders of Naboth's town to hold a meeting, at which two hired false witnesses would appear to accuse Naboth of cursing God. Everything transpired as Jezebel had ordered, and Naboth was stoned to death. Ahab then claimed the vineyard, but at a terrible price: the prophet Isaiah confronted him with the news that his kingdom would be destroyed. (See 1 Kings 21:1-22.)

LEFT FOR DEAD

The apostle Paul endured many physical hardships in his years of ministry, but none perhaps as harrowing as his near-death experience in Lystra. Rounded up by an angry mob stirred to action by Jewish opponents, Paul was dragged outside the city gates and stoned. Left for dead, Paul revived as fellow believers gathered around him. He went back into the city and resumed his travels the next day. (See Acts 14:19-20.)

HOLY VENGEANCE

Scripture outlines the fate of families, nations, and peoples who died defying or neglecting the power of God.

Group	Fact / Reference
Ahab's family	Jehu exterminated the last of Ahab's relatives, in accordance with Isaiah's prophecy *2 Kings 10:1-17*
Amalekites	Crushed by Saul's army for their repeated hostility toward Israel *1 Samuel 15:1-5*
Amorites	Decimated by ferocious hailstorm for opposing the Israelites *Joshua 10:11*
70 men of Beth Shemesh	Died after looking into the Ark of the Covenant *1 Samuel 6:19*
A captain and 50 men	Consumed by fire from heaven for confronting the prophet Elijah *2 Kings 1:9-12*
Ethiopians	Destroyed for attacking Asa, king of Judah *2 Chronicles 14:12*
The firstborn of the Egyptians	Perished because Pharaoh would not allow the Israelites to leave Egypt *Exodus 11:1-10*
Egyptian soldiers	Drowned in the Red Sea in vain attempt to recapture the Israelites *Exodus 14:27-28*
Israelites	Killed by a plague resulting from widespread complaint about their food *Numbers 11:31-35*
Israelites	Killed by poisonous snakebites; the cause once again was complaints about Moses' leadership *Numbers 21:4-6*
10 Israelite spies	Fell ill and died from a plague after delivering fearful reports about the Promised Land *Numbers 14:37*
3,000 Israelites	Executed by the Levites for worshiping a golden calf *Exodus 32:27-28*

70,000 Israelites	Swept by a plague after David ordered a census contrary to God's commands *2 Samuel 24:10-16*
Korah and his followers	Swallowed by the earth for rebelling against Moses' authority *Numbers 26:10*
Moabites and Ammonites	Long-standing enemies of Judah, they killed each other off in a flurry of confusion *2 Chronicles 20:22-23*
Philistines	Killed by tumors and plagues after seizing the Ark of the Covenant *1 Samuel 5:1-12*
1,000 Philistines	Struck dead by Samson in an amazing show of strength *Judges 15:14-15*
Sodomites	Obliterated for their corruption and evil *Genesis 19:24*

STRANGE BUT TRUE

The Handwriting's on the Wall

Mysterious fingers spell doom for a Babylonian king

A human hand suddenly appeared from nowhere! When they saw it, King Belshazzar and his royal guests stared in disbelief. The eerie fingers starting writing on the palace wall, and the king was paralyzed with fear.

He couldn't understand the strange words, but the powerful king of ancient Babylon shuddered with a sense of impending doom. He turned pale as a ghost, his knees knocked together, and his legs became like rubber and gave way beneath him.

Earlier that evening, those same walls rang with riotous laughter and music as King Belshazzar hosted a great feast for a thousand nobles, his court, and his family. As the party got louder and the wine flowed freely, he ordered his servants to bring in the gold and silver cups that his predecessor, King Nebuchadnezzar, had taken from the

Temple in Jerusalem. Filled with wine and a sense of his own importance, King Belshazzar led his guests as they filled the cups with wine and drank toasts from them while they praised their idols of bronze, iron, wood, and stone.

But the party came to an abrupt halt when the hand appeared and wrote these puzzling words: *MENE, MENE, TEKEL, PARSIN*. The king called for his fortune-tellers and astrologers, but none of them could explain the strange words or the mysterious hand that wrote them. They were as mystified as everyone else.

Then someone remembered a young man named Daniel, who was known for his ability to interpret dreams and visions. King Belshazzar had Daniel brought in and asked him to interpret the writing on the palace wall. Daniel agreed and told the king the meaning of the words.

Where did the hand come from? What did the words mean, and who caused them to be written on the wall? Was the king's death—that very evening—connected in any way to the handwriting or to his drinking wine from the cups from the Temple?

Of course, everyone had an opinion about what happened. Most people thought the hand wasn't real but was just blurred vision and an overactive imagination caused from drinking too much wine. As for King Belshazzar's death that same night? Well, that was just a coincidence, they said. Just bad luck! But was it?

Daniel's own explanation was just as amazing. Because the king had defiled the sacred cups and had praised the idols, Daniel said, the hand brought a message of judgment from God.

Daniel told the king: *"Mene* means 'numbered'—God has numbered the days of your reign and has brought it to an end. *Tekel* means 'weighed'—you have been weighed on the balances and have failed the test. *Parsin* means 'divided'—your kingdom has been divided and given to the Medes and Persians." With those words, Daniel predicted the downfall of Belshazzar. Later that same night, King Belshazzar was assassinated, and Darius the Mede occupied the once-mighty city of Babylon.

For more information, read Daniel 5.

POISON-PEN LETTERS

The people who received these messages were not likely hanging around their mailboxes waiting for them. The recipients learned they would suffer punishment, persecution, or death. Read how these grim letters predicted the end of kingdoms and rulers—or boomeranged on their senders.

THE BURNT SCROLL

King Jehoiakim and the people of Judah had reveled in idol worship and persistent immorality. The prophet Jeremiah composed a scroll warning Judah of the disasters that awaited them. Incensed by what he had heard, Jehoiakim burned the scroll in sections. So Jeremiah penned a second scroll, this time condemning Jehoiakim and predicting a disgraceful death for him and his attendants. Jeremiah's words came to pass. Jerusalem was sacked by Babylon's King Nebuchadnezzar, and Jehoiakim died in captivity as he was being transported to Babylon. His son was killed as well. (See Jeremiah 22; 36.)

RIGHT IN THE GUTS

Jehoram, king of Judah during the time of the prophet Elijah, was an evil man. He received a letter from Elijah condemning him for marrying a woman who worshiped idols, murdering his six brothers, and encouraging prostitution and idol worship among his people. The letter predicted that his possessions, sons, and wives would be taken away. The letter also said that Jehoram would die from a lingering disease of the bowels. Shortly after Jehoram received the letter, the Philistines attacked Judah and took away everything he owned, including his sons and wives. Within two years, he died of the debilitating illness Elijah spoke of. He passed away, to no one's regret. (See 2 Chronicles 21.)

THE LETTER THAT BACKFIRED

Sennacherib had brought Assyria to unrivaled power and glory. Naturally, he expected little opposition from tiny Judah, for he had subdued much larger kingdoms. He sent a daunting letter to Hezekiah, king of Judah, telling him that resistance was futile. Sennacherib even declared that the Lord had told him to destroy Judah! Hezekiah tore his clothing and prayed earnestly for deliverance. Isaiah then comforted Hezekiah with a prophecy of victory. That night, almost 200,000 Assyrian soldiers perished in a mysterious plague. Sennacherib returned to his land in disgrace and was later murdered by two of his sons. (See Isaiah 36–37.)

STRANGE BUT TRUE

The King's Last Boast

Herod's death is plagued by more questions than answers

It was daybreak in Caesarea. The first rays of the sun peeped over the horizon. Orange, amber, and red streaked across the dark blue skies. Everyone had gathered—from lesser known officials to the important provincial governors of Tyre and Sidon. Supposedly they had come to celebrate Caesar's birthday. But many were driven by an ulterior motive—the opportunity to flatter Herod Agrippa I. The provinces of Tyre and Sidon were dependent on Galilee and Judea for food, and Herod was threatening that lifeline. He was a cruel and conniving man, indulging in an extravagant, careless lifestyle—not even shrinking from masterminding his own brother-in-law's downfall. The officials from Tyre and Sidon knew they had to massage Herod's considerable ego in order for their tiny provinces to survive.

Dramatically Herod made his appearance. In his usual extravagant way, he strutted onto the platform, clothed in a robe made of fine silver. The early morning rays fell on it, making it shine and glitter. What a sight! And what an opportunity for flattery! As one, the people dutifully shouted: "Before we honored you as a man, but now . . . we know you're no mere mortal. Oh, hail Herod." With a self-satisfied grin, Herod drank in their praise.

Suddenly, with the loud cries of the people still ringing in his ears, Herod doubled over in severe pain. He was quickly rushed off by his attendants. Five days later, he died.

What happened on that fateful day? Did the officials of Tyre poison Herod? Or was Herod's sudden death evidence of God's immediate judgment?

The questions abound. And with each answer come more puzzling details. Josephus, a Jewish historian in the first century, reports that at the moment Herod was struck by pain, he saw a strange-looking owl sitting on a rope above his head. Almost a decade earlier when Herod languished in prison (for some foolish comments in front of the Roman emperor), a fellow prisoner had sternly warned that if Herod ever saw an owl again it would be an omen of his impending death.

Luke, the author of Acts, connects Herod's death not to omens or owls but to the angel of the Lord. On that tragic morning, Herod had accepted praise that only God deserved. God responded by sending a mysterious messenger of doom to mete out immediate judgment, leaving Herod to spend his last remaining hours writhing in pain from "worms," a condition diagnosed by medical doctors today as tapeworms.

Herod's untimely death reminds one of the words of Solomon: "Pride goes before destruction, and haughtiness before a fall" (Proverbs 16:18). In this case, the fall was orchestrated by God himself.

For more information, see Acts 12.

THE CUP OF WRATH

Prophets sometimes foretold the fate of entire nations. Yet few prophecies were as sweeping as the series of judgments on the nations that Jeremiah announced shortly before 600 B.C. These predictions and their uncanny outcomes are described in the chart below.

Nation under Judgment	Outcome
Egypt (Jeremiah 46:1-28)	The Egyptian Pharaoh Neco lost a decisive battle at Carchemish in 605 B.C. With that defeat, Egypt's power in the Middle East waned, and Babylon became the dominant power of the region.
Philistia (Jeremiah 47:1-7)	The independence of the Philistine city-states declined as Assyria, Babylon, and then Greece swept through their land. The Maccabees conquered the remnants of this people in the second century B.C.
Moab (Jeremiah 48:1-47)	Nebuchadnezzar occupied their land and effectively destroyed the nation in the years after 600 B.C.
Ammon (Jeremiah 49:1-6)	A constant foe of Israel, Ammon was likely absorbed by the invading Babylonians, though no definite date is recorded.
Edom (Jeremiah 49:7-22)	Edom, whose ancestor was Esau, brother of Jacob, incurred judgment for its cruelty to Israel. It came under the domination of Babylon, Persia, and later Greece and eventually disappeared.
Damascus (Jeremiah 49:23-27)	Nebuchadnezzar defeated and occupied the city around 605 B.C.
Kedar and Hazor (Jeremiah 49:28-33)	Kedar and Hazor were nomadic tribes that lived in the wilderness of the Middle East. Their relative seclusion offered no protection against the invading Babylonians.
Elam (Jeremiah 49:34-39)	Elam would be conquered by Babylon but would rise again. Its chief city, Susa, became the center of the Medo-Persian Empire after Babylon's decline.
Babylon (Jeremiah 50-51)	Jeremiah told the people of Judah that Babylon would be God's agent for judging their sin, but that Babylon itself would be judged. Jeremiah also predicted the return of the exiles from captivity.

TRAGIC ENDS TO TWISTED TYRANTS

Life is not always fair, but some people in the Bible clearly reaped what they sowed. At times it seemed as if the more despotic a leader was, the more horrible his fate.

HE WHO LIVES BY THE SWORD

Saul, the first king of the Israelites, began his reign with God's blessing but wound up a paranoid despot. His brutal end came as he fought the Philistines, the Israelites' most hated enemy. The battle had not gone well. His sons had been killed, and he had been mortally wounded. Like Abimelech, Saul ordered his armor bearer to kill him so the Philistines would not capture and torture him. But Saul's attendant refused, and the king fell on his own sword. (See 1 Samuel 31:1-10; 1 Chronicles 10.)

A CHINK IN HIS ARMOR

Ahab, a weak and often treacherous king of Israel, could not escape the death the prophet Elijah had predicted for him. As Ahab engaged the army of Aram, he disguised himself so he would not draw fire from enemy archers. But a warrior drew his bow and unwittingly struck Ahab in a vulnerable spot in his armor. He died a slow, painful death. Later, his chariot was washed at a pool where prostitutes bathed. As Elijah had foretold, dogs then came and licked up his blood. (See 1 Kings 22:29-38.)

DOG FOOD

If Ahab was the most despicable king in a long line of godless monarchs, Jezebel, his wife, was a most fitting companion. Her crimes included the murder of Naboth and theft of his vineyard, and persecution of God's prophets, including Elijah. After Ahab's death, Jezebel's son, Joram, became king. His life and reign were cut short by Jehu, the man anointed to avenge Ahab's crimes. Jezebel in turn suffered a gruesome demise. Jehu marched to Jezreel and ordered the queen's eunuchs to throw her out of a high window, where she fell to her death. Hours later Jehu's men went out to bury Jezebel's body, but all they could find were her skull, her feet, and her hands. Dogs had consumed most of her remains. (See 2 Kings 9:30-37.)

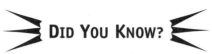

DID YOU KNOW?

What is the strange land whose identity still eludes scholars and laypeople alike?

In the book of Genesis (10:2), the land of Magog is grouped with Meshech and Tubal, regions near present-day Turkey. Magog looms large in the prophetic visions of both Ezekiel and John, but the exact location of Magog remains shrouded in mystery. Ezekiel seems to use the names Gog and Magog as a metaphor for vast armies who will invade Israel from the north in the end times (Ezekiel 38:1-9). They are bloodthirsty enemies of God (Ezekiel 38:14-23). These geographic references led a number of popular authors and speakers during the Cold War to equate Gog and Magog with the Soviet Union. The book of Revelation, while less specific than Ezekiel, uses Gog and Magog to describe peoples deceived by Satan who willingly do his bidding (Revelation 20:8).

STRANGE BUT TRUE

Ghost Town

Why was a curse placed on a thriving ancient city?

In recent times, we have seen cities and towns evacuated and leveled because of toxic contamination of the soil. Yet an ancient city was once leveled and abandoned because of its spiritual contamination. Of all the cities in the world, it was the only one cursed in the entire Old Testament.

Jericho fell (literally) into Israelite hands when Joshua obeyed the command of the Lord to do his now-famous seven-day march around the city walls. The walls fell at the blast of trumpets, and the city was destroyed. Joshua then promised that anyone who attempted to rebuild the ruins would experience a curse: "At the cost of his firstborn son, he will lay its foundation. At the cost of his youngest son, he will set up its gates."

Such words did not bother Hiel of Bethel, who during the debauched reign of King Ahab attempted to rebuild the great Canaanite city. Yet Joshua's curse struck his family with deadly accuracy: His firstborn son Abiram and youngest son Segub died during his reconstruction of the city.

Why would such an unusual curse be applied to a conquered city that had lots of economic potential and was now in Israelite hands? Surely the people could make good use of prime real estate. Why the clench-fisted rule outlawing any development?

Some have suggested that the curse pointed to the irrevocable difference between God's blessing on people who obey him and his judgment against those who do not. Jericho would remain a pile of rocks (though Israelites did populate the immediate region) as a symbol that the God who blesses also curses—fair warning to people who take God for granted.

So if you travel today to the Jordan River basin and walk down from sea level to the place of old Jericho, you'll still see a heap, though now it's an earthen mound, not a rock pile.

To read more about Jericho and its curse, see Joshua 6. For the fate of Hiel, see 1 Kings 16:34.

CURIOUS CONNECTIONS

URBAN DECAY
Cities, like the people who live in them, grow and decline. Some prosper, while others pass away quietly. But some cities expire suddenly, carried away by war, famine, or disease. The Bible records the fate of immoral cities that ignored God's warnings and collapsed in ruin.

SODOM AND GOMORRAH
Lust, rape, perversion, obscene and vile addictions . . . Sodom and Gomorrah housed all that was evil. The God of Israel could not find

even five good people in the whole city of Sodom! Before totally destroying the cities, God's angels had to drag Lot, his two daughters, and his wife out of Sodom. They were warned not to look back as the cities burned. Lot's wife disregarded this command and glanced at Sodom. She turned instantly into a pillar of salt. The burning pitch and sulfur from the skies destroyed not only the cities but also the entire plain and all the vegetation of the land. Abraham, living nearby, could see the smoke rising from the ruins. (See Genesis 18–19.)

NINEVEH

Idolatry, prostitution, witchcraft, exploitation of the helpless, and cruelty in war were only some of the evils practiced in the ancient city of Nineveh. Jonah was sent by the God of Israel to condemn this great Assyrian city. He proclaimed that the city would be destroyed in forty days! Remarkably, the Ninevites believed Jonah's message! All of them, young and old, poor and rich, fasted and pleaded with the God of Israel. Even the king proclaimed that all the people should put aside their wickedness and call on God. Jonah's God heard their pleas and had mercy on the people. Nineveh's reform did not last long, however. One hundred years later, God sent the prophet Nahum to pronounce judgment again on the city. The people spurned God's message this time. Within a few decades, the mighty Assyrian Empire was crushed by the Babylonians. (See Jonah 1–3 and the book of Nahum.)

BABYLON

The raucous celebration had begun! Rising to the heavens in a phenomenal feat of will and imagination, the great Tower of Babel filled human hearts with pride and self-satisfaction. Because it struck such a defiant gesture against God's sovereignty, God sought to confuse the language of this civilization so that such pride would be forever hindered. Much later, Babylon continued to defy God. The prophet Isaiah declared that Babylon's rise would be heady but short-lived. Its destruction would be complete; it would never be inhabited through all generations. Today the ancient city lies in ruin, buried under mounds of dirt and sand in present-day Iraq. (See Genesis 11.)

◪ HEAVEN AND HELL

The pit, the Lake of Fire, the second death—these are the vivid images that the Bible associates with hell. On the other hand, Scripture also gives us a glimpse of the beauty and peace of heaven. Even so, our understanding of the afterlife is cloaked in mystery. What facts does the Bible disclose about the eternal destiny of the human race?

FACTS ABOUT HELL
1. It is engulfed in darkness (Matthew 25:30; 2 Peter 2:17).
2. It is a place of suffering and thirst (Luke 16:19-31).
3. Fire burns in it day and night (Matthew 18:8; Mark 9:43).
4. It is a place of punishment for the spiritually indifferent or neglectful (Matthew 25:46).
5. Those present in hell are separated from God (2 Thessalonians 1:7-9).
6. It is likened to a lake of fire, a place of torment for Satan and his angels (Revelation 20:14).

FACTS ABOUT HEAVEN
1. It will be a place prepared by God for his children (John 14:2-3).
2. The redeemed will resemble Jesus (John 14:9).
3. The human body will be renewed and perfected (John 20:19, 26; 1 Corinthians 15:35-49).
4. Human relationships will be transformed, and marriage will cease (Matthew 22:29-32).
5. Sorrow and mourning will disappear, and tears will no longer flow (Revelation 21:4).
6. The heavenly city exudes beauty and wonder (Revelation 21).
7. God's brilliant presence so fills heaven that there is no need for light or the sun (Revelation 21:23).
8. Death will be abolished (Revelation 21:4).

Swallowed Alive

Conspirators, fire, earthquakes, and the plague

Slowly the Israelites backed away from the desert tents belonging to Korah, Dathan, and Abiram. These men had come out and were standing with their wives and children, when suddenly the earth began to tremble. The ground beneath the families split apart, and the earth opened its mouth and swallowed them, their households, and all their possessions. Screaming, they tumbled alive into a yawning grave.

Filled with fear, the rest of the Israelites fled to their own tents. But then from out of nowhere, a raging fire rose and licked up 250 more men. Smoke and the smell of burning flesh filled the air. Why did this happen? According to the Scriptures, those ancient Israelite nomads asked the same questions many of us ask today: Why did God strike down these people?

The day before this calamity, Korah, Dathan, and Abiram had challenged Aaron and Moses. They accused Moses and Aaron of placing themselves above all the people, lording over them as great high priests. According to these challengers, everyone had a right to approach God and the sacred objects of the Tabernacle on an equal footing. But now these defiant challengers of the status quo and their followers were dead. The people could not help but cringe in fear as they remembered the words of Moses that still rang in their ears: "It is against the God of Israel that you grumble! Not against Aaron, or me. In the morning, the God of Israel will show who belongs to him and who is holy." That morning, the earth opened its mouth and swallowed Korah, Dathan, and Abiram alive.

The Israelites fumed and fretted about this disaster. Why did these men have to die? What did they do wrong? But blaming Moses and Aaron and continuing to challenge the authority given to them by God only brought more horror. Soon afterward, a plague ravaged the camp, killing scores more. By the time it was all over, the twelve clans of Israel had been decimated. The decomposing bodies were stacked outside the camp. Everyone knew of a father or mother, brother or sister who had succumbed to the plague.

Those who rush to the conclusion that the Israelites were victims of an angry God overlook the patience the Israelites had been afforded. They had seen the plagues that had ruined Egypt but had not touched them; they had witnessed the Red Sea collapsing around the pursuing Egyptian armies; they had had their food and water provided daily. Seeking only their own pleasure and comfort, they had repeatedly turned away from divine guidance. The divine judgments can thus be seen as the sad but fitting end of a stubborn, rebellious generation.

For more information, read Numbers 16.

CuRiOuS CoNNEcTiONS

LISTEN UP!
God proclaimed the seriousness of his judgments in remarkable ways. His prophets relied on dramatic and memorable gestures to make sure God's voice was heard. Some listened; others suffered the consequences.

THE NAKED TRUTH
In the book of Isaiah, God accuses Egypt and Ethiopia of serious crimes. He announces that their people will be led away naked, slaves of the king of Assyria. To emphasize his point, he had his prophet Isaiah remain naked for three years. In Middle Eastern culture, nakedness invited terrible humiliation—the kind of shame God's enemies would endure. (See Isaiah 20.)

GRUNGE CLOTHING
God told the prophet Jeremiah to buy a linen belt and put it around his waist. That was unremarkable, but then God told him to take the belt and hide it in a rocky crevice. After a long time, Jeremiah dug up the belt, which was now rotted and ruined. Thus the people of Judah and Jerusalem would see how God would use Babylon to rot away their pride like the worthless belt. (See Jeremiah 13:1-11.)

YOKE OF OPPRESSION

A yoke is a heavy, cumbersome object put on the shoulders of oxen to control and steer them. The prophet Jeremiah couldn't have been thrilled when God told him to put a yoke on his own shoulders as a message to his people and the neighboring peoples that they must serve their conqueror, King Nebuchadnezzar, and follow his direction just as a beast obeys the turn of its yoke. (See Jeremiah 27–28.)

EGO TRIP

Nebuchadnezzar, the king of Babylon, had become quite impressed with himself. So much did he wallow in his accomplishments that he came to believe that he alone had been responsible for his greatness. As Daniel tells us, Nebuchadnezzar was suddenly forced from his palace. His kingdom was taken away from him for seven years, and a mental illness caused him to eat grass and live like a wild animal. Only after his insanity lifted and he realized that God is in control of all earthly kingdoms and chooses their rulers did Nebuchadnezzar pray to God, who restored his mind. (See Daniel 4:28-38.)

DID YOU KNOW?

What ferocious beast mentioned in the Bible has defied scientific classification?

In the book of Job we meet the strange creature called the Leviathan. Having rows of shields on its back, scales as sharp as glass on its underside, and fearsome, sharp teeth, it struck fear in human hearts. This beast of the sea (the Hebrew word for Leviathan means literally "sea serpent") was said to also spurt fire and smoke from its mouth and nose (Job 41:1-34, NIV).

Many Bible commentators have suggested that the Leviathan is an exaggerated description of the crocodile, the hyperbole being a Hebrew literary technique to emphasize the strength of this reptile. Others have suggested that the Leviathan might be some kind of fierce dinosaur from the ancient past. Some scholars have noted the remarkable similarities between the descriptions of the Leviathan in the Bible and the Lotan, an evil, seven-headed sea monster prevalent in ancient Canaanite lore (see Psalm 74:14). These commentators have suggested that the multiheaded, fire-breathing Leviathan is a primitive symbol of chaos and depravity.

Whether these extraordinary descriptions of a multiheaded monster actually resembled some huge serpent that roamed the ancient seas remains unknown. But what *is* known is that this beast became a powerful image of evil, for the book of Revelation alludes to a seven-headed sea monster who will wreak havoc on the earth in the last days (Revelation 13:1-9).

STRANGE BUT TRUE

Firstborn, First to Die

The last of the plagues on Egypt was the worst

Pharaoh had seen the Nile turn to a river of blood. He had walked on a land covered with frogs, then gnats, flies, and finally locusts. He had watched livestock fall down dead and boils cover his people. Hailstones and then great darkness had descended on his kingdom. All these things had come through the hand of Moses.

So did Pharaoh not believe the threat on his nation's firstborn sons when he again refused to allow Moses and the Israelites to leave Egypt?

It was at midnight that the firstborn males—animals as well as humans—were struck dead because of Pharaoh's hard-heartedness. They died mysteriously and without warning. The biblical account of the tragedy is more direct. It reveals that the firstborn were struck down by the Lord, killed by an angel of death that passed over the land. Yet just as mysterious is the fact that a select few of the firstborn males living in Egypt were spared.

Who survived? And why? The children of the Israelites were not killed; their parents had followed the strange instructions communicated to them by Moses and Aaron. They took perfect male lambs, slaughtered them at twilight, and wiped some of the blood on the sides and tops of the door frames. They roasted and ate the meat with bitter herbs and bread made without yeast and eaten in haste.

When God's hand of death moved over the land, it passed over the homes marked with the lamb's blood. That night Pharaoh finally released the Israelites from a history of 430 years of slavery, and they left the country as quickly as they could. To this day Jews celebrate Passover to remember the night that God's final plague passed over their homes.

The complete account of the Passover can be found in Exodus 11–12.

CURIOUS CONNECTIONS

UNLUCKY SEVENTIES
The Bible records a few incidents in which scores of people are killed by war, plague, or murder. Curiously, three of these stories have the same number of victims—70. The following connections highlight the tragic histories of these people, who were in the wrong place at the wrong time.

A VIEW TO DIE FOR
The Ark of the Covenant—the sacred container of God's covenant with Israel—had been seized in battle by the Philistines. Naturally, Israel was overjoyed by the Ark's return some time later to the village of Beth-shemesh. Out of curiosity or carelessness, the men of the village looked inside the Ark, a brazen gesture God equated with entering the holiest place unworthily. As a result, 70 people died, causing fear and mourning throughout Israel. (See 1 Samuel 6:19-20.)

SEVENTY HEADS
Jehu, king of Israel during the time of the prophet Elisha, was commanded by the prophet to destroy the house of the former King Ahab. Ahab had 70 sons and numerous close relatives. Jehu sent the guardians of Ahab's children a letter that told them to pick the best son, set him on his father's throne, and prepare to defend themselves.

The guardians, administrators, and chief men of the palace were frightened. They replied that they would not make anyone king and would do whatever Jehu said. So Jehu sent a second letter, which told them to take the heads of the 70 sons, put them in baskets, and stack them in two piles on either side of the entrance to the city gate. They obeyed the letter but were then killed themselves. Jehu continued his bloodbath until all remaining relatives and close acquaintances of Ahab were wiped from the face of the earth. (See 2 Kings 10:1-17.)

THE MURDEROUS HEIR
The offspring of the judge Gideon and a concubine, Abimelech aspired to rule over Shechem. Upon his father's death, Abimelech approached the leaders of Shechem and won their support for his plan. Not satisfied with their approval, Abimelech took it upon himself to murder his 70 half brothers in order to eliminate any future threat. But one brother, Jotham, got away and called down a curse on Abimelech as he was being crowned. Jotham's curse came to pass when Abimelech was killed during the siege of Thebez. (See Judges 9.)

CURIOUS CONNECTIONS

INSTANT LEPROSY
God's great patience was sorely tested by those who angered him or defied his commands. Sometimes he used illness or affliction to change cold hearts or to end rebellion. In the case of Moses, God used an illness to demonstrate his mastery over all nature. Scripture relates a few episodes of "instant leprosy" that struck without warning.

A SIGN FROM GOD
God had just revealed his plan of redemption to Moses. Fearful and confused, Moses blurted out his concern that no one would believe that God had chosen him. So God gave him two signs—his staff, which could turn into a serpent and back again, and his own hand. When Moses placed his hand under his robe and removed it again, it was leprous—as white as snow! But when he placed his hand

inside the robe a second time, the hand returned to normal. God told Moses to use these signs before the people of Israel so they would know he had sent Moses to lead them. (See Exodus 4:1-8.)

A JEALOUS SISTER

Moses was the leader of his people, and his sister, Miriam, enjoyed a great deal of status as a worship leader. Still, she expressed jealousy of Moses' unchallenged leadership and teamed with her brother Aaron to criticize Moses' marriage to a foreign woman. God heard her complaint and chastised her for her attitude. To punish Miriam, God inflicted her with leprosy for seven days—an affliction that forced her to remain outside the Israelite camp until she was pronounced clean. (See Numbers 12:1-15.)

PRIDE GOETH BEFORE A FALL

Uzziah had been a good king, but he became proud of his power. One day he disobeyed God by going into the Temple and burning an incense offering to God, which was the duty of the priests. Because of this, Uzziah was stricken with leprosy for the remainder of his life. That meant he could never again enter the Temple or even his own palace. His son had to rule in his place. When Uzziah died, he could not be buried in the royal tombs because of his disease. (See 2 Chronicles 26:16-23.)

THE SEVEN SEALS OF REVELATION

The seven seals that are opened in the book of Revelation are one of the most well-known symbols of judgment and apocalypse in all literature. The symbolism has appeared in art and prose throughout the centuries. But what do the seals mean?

Seal / Symbol	Description / Reference	Possible Meaning
First Seal: The White Horse	Its rider wears a crown and carries a bow. He marches out to seek victory in battle. *Revelation 6:1-2*	Many scholars have concluded that it stands for the outbreak of violence in the coming Tribulation.
Second Seal: The Red Horse	Its rider is given a large sword and has the power and authority to take peace from the earth. *Revelation 6:3-4*	The red horse symbolizes a judgment of killing and warfare, accompanied by other disasters.
Third Seal: The Black Horse	Its rider holds a pair of scales while proclaiming the dearth of food and wine. *Revelation 6:5-6*	The black horse symbolizes the panic and misery caused by famine.
Fourth Seal: The Pale Horse	The rider's name is Death and its cohort, the Grave. They inflict suffering and death on a quarter of the world's population. *Revelation 6:7-8*	The pale horse is death in various brutal forms.
Fifth Seal: The Souls under the Altar	On and beneath the altar were the souls of those who had been killed for preaching God's Word. *Revelation 6:9-11*	The events of the fifth seal, unlike the previous four, take place in the realm of the spirit. The breaking of the seal announces God's vindication of saints who have suffered persecution.
Sixth Seal: The Great Earthquake	The earth is overwhelmed with natural calamities, each so devastating that people flee to escape God's wrath. *Revelation 6:12-17*	The earthquake reveals the wrath of the Lamb, whose anger cannot be withstood. Humans choose to be crushed by mountains rather than face the One they have rejected.
Seventh Seal: Silence in Heaven	The opening of the seal begins with a long silence in heaven but culminates with seven judgments. *Revelation 8:1*	The seventh seal begins the final cycle of judgments that ushers in the final battle between Christ and the forces of darkness.

DID YOU KNOW?

What is the "abomination of desolation"?

In the book of Daniel and in the Gospels, we find mention of the "abomination of desolation" that will appear in Jerusalem's Temple during the last days. For centuries Bible students have debated the meaning of this phrase. Some have suggested that it refers to vainglorious rulers such as Antiochus Epiphanes who attempted to deify themselves, or to the emperor Titus, who destroyed the Temple and much of Jerusalem in A.D. 70. Others see the phrase as a metaphor for the unsuccessful attempts of heathenism to undo the spiritual victory of Jesus over Satan. Those who hold to premillennial theology posit the meaning in the future, during a time of complete lawlessness before Christ's return. (See Daniel 11:31 and Matthew 24:15.)

 FAQs (frequently asked questions)

FIRE AND BRIMSTONE

You can't expect me to believe in a place where horned devils jab people with pitchforks. Is that what the Bible says about hell?

Many of the popular images of hell are often misinformed. Complicating the issue is the language used in the Bible to describe hell—are we to take such images literally, or are they devices that convey the misery of such a place? We can reach some conclusions, however. Clearly hell is a place of torment and suffering. Peter describes hell as containing "gloomy caves" that hold those awaiting judgment (2 Peter 2:4). Jesus referred to hell several times, calling it a place of "unquenchable fires" (Mark 9:43).

Does the Bible tell about anyone who went to hell?

In his first epistle, Peter tells us that Jesus suffered a physical death and "preached to the spirits in prison"—perhaps a reference to a liberation of hell (see 1 Peter 3:19). However, the parable of

Lazarus and the rich man (Luke 16:19-31) tells the story of a soul in torment. The rich man's sin was neglect of God and of his neighbor, the beggar Lazarus. In hell, he finds himself engulfed in flames, writhing with an unquenchable thirst. He is able to see Lazarus being comforted in heaven by Abraham. A great chasm divides hell from heaven, and the souls in one place cannot cross over to the other.

What is Sheol?

Sheol is a Hebrew word commonly translated as "the pit" or "the grave." In Old Testament writings, Sheol harbored the souls of the dead and was thought to be deep in the earth itself. Although it is variously described as "Death and Destruction" (Proverbs 27:20) and "a land of darkness and utter gloom" (Job 10:21), it was not a place of punishment but rather the destiny of all human souls. Several passages in the Old Testament describe God's power to raise souls from Sheol and hint at the Christian understanding of the afterlife.

What is brimstone, and why is it associated with hell?

Brimstone is a natural form of sulfur, a yellowish mineral that easily ignites and burns. Brimstone can be found today near and around the Dead Sea. Its association with divine judgment likely comes from the fate of Sodom and Gomorrah, destroyed by a heavenly rain of "fire and burning sulfur" (Genesis 19:24). The book of Revelation also pictures the punishment by fire and burning sulphur of those who worship the Antichrist (Revelation 14:10).

COLLECTIVE JUDGMENTS

Did God really want the Israelites to kill off other people?

Some passages in the Bible contain specific commands for the Israelites to wipe out entire populations. In Numbers 31, for instance,
we read of a campaign of vengeance against the Midianites that
spared practically no one. The people of Canaan had become so
immersed in sin that they posed a dangerous influence on the
morality of the nation of Israel.

Why do some of the psalms seem to rejoice in the destruction and suffering of enemies?

Sometimes called the *imprecatory* psalms, these hymns request
God's help in destroying an enemy. A good example is Psalm 109, in
which the author implores God to make "his children become father-
less, and . . . his wife become a widow" (Psalm 109:9). Although
seemingly cruel, the point of such psalms is often missed. Rather
than rely on his own power, the speaker trusts in God to carry out
justice that is perfect and appropriate. This theme appears in all the
imprecatory psalms. God will aid those who are right and just, not
those who simply wish to settle a score with an enemy.

I find it hard to understand why entire families would be executed for the actions of one person. Can you explain this?

In 2 Samuel 21, we read the account of seven relatives of Saul who
were executed for no crime on their part. Their forebear, long since
dead, had killed a number of Gibeonites who were supposed to be
protected according to an oath made with Israel. Thus Saul had in-
curred *bloodguilt* on himself and his house for his violation of this
oath. Bloodguilt allowed a family of a victim to exact retribution,
even taking the killer's life if the deed was premeditated. The customs of the day also allowed for relatives of the killer to be put to
death under certain circumstances, especially if the crime had not
been addressed or punished adequately.

If the Israelites were God's chosen people, why did they suffer so much oppression?
Israel's history reached lofty heights and fell to abysmal pits. Times of great achievement were followed by captivity and abject desolation. The writers of Scripture usually identified oppression with disobedience to God's law. The Babylonian captivity of 586 B.C., according to Jeremiah, was a direct result of Israel's flirting with idolatry and refusal to listen to God's prophets. The times of exile, harsh as they were, were meant to bring the people back to their foundations—a pure, holy life centered in God.

THREE

SINISTER SCHEMES

Encounters with the Wicked and Demonic

Hog Wild

What caused thousands of pigs to go berserk?

One hot, dry day in ancient Israel, livestock contentedly grazed near a hillside graveyard. Standing nearby were Jesus and another man, a disturbed vagrant who had terrorized the local populace for years. When Jesus motioned to the herd of swine, all 2,000 of the prized pigs—to the herdsmen's amazement—frantically ran off the side of a mountain and into the lake below, where they all drowned. Horrified and angry, the herdsmen realized they had suffered a catastrophic financial blow.

What in the world was going on? At first glance it appeared that this Jewish rabbi was judging those who made a living raising livestock forbidden by the law of Moses. Pork was not kosher. What wasn't so clear, however, was how Jesus had evoked such amazing power over the pigs. Was it a case of mass hypnosis? Could the rabbi from Nazareth throw his voice like a ventriloquist? If so, perhaps the pigs were responding to what they thought was a herdsmen's voice on the other side of the cliff. Maybe it had nothing to do with Jesus. It's possible that a wild animal in the brush had startled one of the herd, provoking hysteria.

The vagrant who had observed it all was beginning to draw his own conclusions. Homeless and deranged, he had lived among the tombstones of the graveyard. The herdsmen and townspeople kept their distance from this obviously crazed hermit. He wore no clothes! This wild man with matted, uncombed hair wondered if it was only coincidental that at the very moment the pigs ran off the side of the mountain, his unclothed body fell limp to the ground? At that very moment he felt a rush of peace wash over his mind and inner spirit. For the first time in decades, his mouth formed a smile as he looked up at Jesus, who returned his smile.

Jesus had diagnosed this man's problem as an extraordinary manifestation of demons. So many had inhabited the man that they called themselves "legion." The Roman term *legion* was a designation for 6,000 soldiers. Obviously an inner army had barricaded themselves in this man's soul, holding him hostage.

When Jesus commanded the legion of demons to come out of the man, the Bible says that the demons begged Jesus to send them into the pigs. Jesus gave the demons permission to enter the pigs, and when the spirits came out of the man and entered the pigs, the pigs (2,000 in all) "plunged down the steep hillside into the lake, where they drowned" (Mark 5:13).

Legend has it that exorcised demons must inhabit another being. It appears this is what happened to the pigs.

The demons that had inhabited the man were now clothed in pigskin. How else could this bizarre set of circumstances be explained?

Study the account in Mark 5:1-20 for details on this puzzling occurrence.

CURIOUS CONNECTIONS

DEMONIC POSSESSION

What exactly constitutes demonic possession? Is is possible for evil spirits to inhabit a person? The New Testament, in particular, records several episodes in which a spiritual force of some sort invades the human body. The possession can appear in many forms, including seizures, violent behavior, self-mutilation, and illness. In these accounts, the torment is relieved when the demons are cast out by a greater spiritual presence.

THE DEMONIC DESPOT

A psychiatrist who examined the mind of King Saul might conclude that he suffered from manic depression or another mental illness. His erratic behavior and sharp mood swings surely indicated a disturbed personality. Over time, the king became obsessed with the rise of David, the talented shepherd whose earnestness and purity outshone Saul's mediocrity. We learn in 1 Samuel 19:9-10 that David was in Saul's house, playing the harp for him. An evil spirit entered Saul, and he hurled a spear at David, narrowly missing him. Saul later attempted to kill his own son Jonathan.

ENOUGH ALREADY!

Some demons apparently were not dangerous but were annoying. A humorous account in Acts tells of Paul and Silas in the city of Philippi being followed by a girl who had a spirit of divination in her, which meant that she had the power to tell the future. The girl followed the men for days, shouting that they were servants of the Most High God and that they were telling how to be saved. Paul finally had enough and turned around and sent the demon out of the girl. The girl's owners were not amused. They had used the girl for making money, so they had Paul and Silas dragged into court. (See Acts 16:16-19.)

NOT FOR THE FAINTHEARTED

One of the more puzzling encounters with demons is recorded in Mark 9. Here Jesus met a man whose son exhibited disturbing behavior—speechlessness, foaming at the mouth, and seizures. The man claimed that Jesus' disciples had tried but failed to expel the demon that had been causing the affliction. After rebuking the crowd for their lack of faith, Jesus ordered the demon to leave. The boy shuddered and collapsed but soon recovered. Later, Jesus told the disciples that the demon they encountered could only be exorcised through prayer. (See Mark 9:14-29.)

DID YOU KNOW?

Why did the ancient Israelites sacrifice their children to Molech in the valley of Hinnom?

Although the valley of Hinnom would eventually become the garbage dump of Jerusalem and a symbol of the corruption of hell, it was first the site of the worship of Molech, the god of the Ammonites. One of the rites associated with the worship of this "detestable god" (1 Kings 11:5) was the sacrifice of live children on a ceremonial fire. Precisely how these innocent children were sacrificed continues to be a fact buried in the distant past. Jewish rabbinic writers give us a clue, though. They describe a series of horrific rites revolving around a hollow bronze statue of a man with an ox's head. Inside this statue was a furious fire that burned to death those innocent victims who were shoved into this death trap. In clear and forceful language, Mosaic law condemned such hideous rites.

STRANGE BUT TRUE

The Prince of Darkness

What does the Bible tell us about Satan?

Universally known as the epitome of evil, Satan appears throughout the Bible in various guises—a cunning serpent, a fallen angel, a threatening demon. He is powerful (though the power he exerts is limited) and fearsome. He longs to destroy what is good—that is, what God has brought forth. Job's prosperous life, for example, was torn asunder by disease, ferocious marauders, terrifying storms, earthquakes, and fire. Satan dragged Job down to the ash pit—literally. Throughout the Bible he appears as a relentless schemer who resorts to lies, fear, and temptations to lure others to a destiny they will share with him—a place of everlasting torment. In fact, his name means "adversary."

Satan's very existence raises a lot of questions. How could a powerful, luminous angel spurn a perfect existence in God's presence? Why would an all-powerful God allow such widespread rebellion? Why does an all-powerful God permit Satan to wield the considerable power he has? And on a purely practical level, what relevance does the devil have for modern humanity? Such questions have been debated endlessly, and the answers remain elusive. But it would be a mistake, as the apologist C. S. Lewis has noted, to dismiss Satan as a quaint relic of a superstitious age. In Scripture, Satan stands at the center of the world's troubles—corrupting, sowing discord, prowling, snaring unsuspecting victims, and masquerading as an angel of light. Jesus clearly declared that he was locked in a mortal struggle with the prince of darkness and that Jesus would emerge victorious.

Satan's biography, if it were taken from the Bible, might begin with his preeminent place among God's creatures before the world began. Some scholars have suggested that Isaiah's description of Lucifer—a name meaning "daystar"—gives us a glimpse of Satan's rise and fall (Isaiah 14:12). He appears in the guise of a serpent in the Garden of Eden (Genesis 3) and as Job's tormentor (Job 1). The writer of the Chronicles declares that Satan coaxed David into taking his ill-advised census (1 Chronicles 21:1).

In the New Testament, Satan's opposition to God becomes bolder. His demons oppress people and resist Jesus' works. He even tries to tempt Jesus (Matthew 4) and enters Judas Iscariot, who betrays Jesus (John 13:27). He vigorously attacks the new church and spreads discord wherever he can. Small wonder that the writers of the New Testament epistles describe him as a formidable opponent (Ephesians 6:11; 1 Peter 5:8).

Satan has wreaked havoc on the world and left a trail of broken lives behind. Yet God has already brought Satan down by the ultimate victory of good—the death and resurrection of the Son of God, the basis for the Easter celebration. The glimpse of the future presented in John's Revelation shows Satan's ultimate demise—everlasting torment in a lake of fire (Revelation 20:7-10).

Many Bible sections deal with Satan. Start your investigation with 1 John 3:8; John 14:30; Ephesians 2:2; 1 Peter 5:8; and 1 Corinthians 7:5.

IDOL HANDS ARE THE DEVIL'S WORKSHOP

Sometimes the most appalling cults sprang from casual indifference and financial greed rather than blatant idolatry. These three stories share that common thread. And in all three cases, tragedy followed. Read about how these "idol" hands fashioned disaster for God's people.

GIDEON'S EPHOD

Gideon had triumphed decisively over two Midianite kings, and his followers wanted to reward him. They offered to let him rule over them. Gideon declined but asked instead for a small portion of gold from each man, which they gladly gave. From this Gideon made an ephod of gold and placed it in his hometown of Ophrah. The ephod—most likely a breastplate—was probably displayed for public viewing. Perhaps influenced by the customs of pagan neighbors, who often venerated such objects as they would idols, the Israelites soon began to worship the ephod itself. The author of Judges comments that the ephod "became a trap for Gideon and his family" (Judges 8:27). Soon after Gideon's death, Israel slid back into idolatry, and Gideon's son Abimelech murdered all of Gideon's remaining sons during a short and violent reign. (See Judges 8:22–9:9.)

MICAH'S IDOLS

During the time of the judges, the Israelites were religiously confused, to say the least. The story of Micah, a well-meaning but misguided man, exemplifies the spiritual poverty of the era. Micah owned a shrine in which he kept an ephod and household idols. He hired a Levite—a member of Israel's priestly line—to serve as his personal priest, believing he would receive a blessing for such piety. Instead, the priest was lured away by a band of warriors from the tribe of Dan, who used the priest as a sort of good-luck charm as they plundered a nearby village. Not only did they take the Levite, but they grabbed the idols too. When Micah protested, the Danites threatened to kill him. So Micah was left with nothing. The warriors then leveled the town of Laish and set up their own shrine to worship the idol. They appointed a descendant of Moses to serve as their priest and maintained the shrine for many years. (See Judges 17:1–18:31.)

THE JEALOUS SILVERSMITH

Demetrius had a bad feeling about the new religion that was winning converts in his city of Ephesus. A silversmith who made a good living making and selling shrines of the goddess Artemis, Demetrius saw big losses and red ink in his financial future. Gathering a number of fellow craftsmen, he stirred them to a fury, blaming the Christians for all their troubles. The rage spread to others in the town, and soon a great riot began. Dragging the apostle Paul's companions to an outdoor theater, the rioters began shouting and protesting incessantly. Soon the scene broke down into utter chaos. Finally, the mayor of Ephesus restored calm, and Paul and his fellow missionaries were able to leave the city unharmed. (See Acts 19:21-40.)

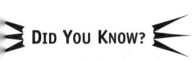

DID YOU KNOW?

Why did the ancient Israelites use the obscure name Beelzebub to refer to Satan?
One of the most peculiar names for Satan, the prince of demons, is the name *Beelzebub* (Mark 3:22). The origins of this obscure word continue to puzzle many Bible scholars. The close association between Beelzebub and the name of an Ekron god, Baal-zebub, seems obvious (2 Kings 1:2). Yet there remain persistent doubts whether Baal-zebub was actually a name for any ancient god. *Baal-zebub* literally means "lord of the flies"—a phrase used by William Golding for the title of his nightmarish 1954 novel. Many scholars believe the real name of this god was Baal-zebul, meaning "Lord of the Heavenly Dwelling." Since the Israelite prophets would not honor any god with such a distinguished title except the God of Israel, they seemed to have substituted a derogatory name,

meaning "Lord of the Flies" or "Lord of Dung," for this god. By Jesus' time, Beelzebub was a common epithet for Satan.

STRANGE BUT TRUE

The Saline Fraulein

What really happened to the woman who looked back at Sodom?

Lot is one of the Bible's most famous husbands, not for anything he did to win points with his wife, but for the distinct and unusual honor of being married to a block of salt. Here's how it happened.

Ancient Sodom crawled with seedy characters. Its name has come to stand for debauchery. Its character was worse than daytime TV soap operas. One night around the year 2050 B.C., Lot was instructed to evacuate the city, for the anger of God was about to fall upon it. He had too little time to arrange for the sale of his residence, but at least he had his life. The one condition: "Don't look back."

So Lot got away before fire poured from heaven on the sorry city of Sodom. And on his family's race out of town, he kept insisting, kept begging, kept warning, "Don't look back!"

But Lot's wife did glance backward, a quick look over the shoulder. After all, these fireworks would never happen again in her lifetime, a lifetime that was to be quite short indeed, for in the next instant, her body became a block of salt. How could such a dramatic chemical change happen so fast?

Maybe she was hit by debris from the firestorm—hot lava that turned her corpse into crystalline salt. Maybe the sight she saw was so scary that her body went berserk, she froze and turned white with fright. A more literal interpretation suggests that God turned her body into an inert block of sodium chloride.

No wonder Lot and the rest of his family moved on hastily and never looked back!

For more on Lot's wife, read Genesis 19.

TWISTED SISTERS

These women are chiefly remembered for their scheming and callousness—but their plans came to naught in the end.

THE JILTED WIFE

Joseph, a fine specimen of a man, had been taken to Egypt in chains and was soon bought by Potiphar, one of Pharaoh's officials. He performed his duties well, but since he was also attractive he caught the eye of Potiphar's wife. She was very direct: "Come to bed with me!" He refused, day after day. Finally, with no one home but her and Joseph, she made one final, desperate bid, but Joseph again rebuffed her. As he ran away, she grabbed his cloak. When Potiphar came home, his wife played the distraught victim. She showed him the cloak as evidence that she had fought off Joseph's advances. The enraged Potiphar threw the innocent Joseph into prison, where he languished for years. (See Genesis 39:1-23.)

KISS AND TELL

Samson was a man consecrated to God, though he certainly had his struggles with pride and anger. He also could not resist an enticing woman, regardless of her upbringing or character. Delilah, a Philistine woman, lived in the valley of Sorek and had caught Samson's eye. The Philistine leaders, who had been humiliated by Samson on many occasions, learned of the romance and convinced her to find out the secret of Samson's strength. Three times she tried in vain to discover his secret, but her nagging eventually wore Samson down. He told her the secret—that his hair had to remain uncut, since he had taken a vow before God. While he was sleeping, the Philistines cut his hair, then tied him up. Delilah's betrayal of her lover was complete. (See Judges 16:1-21.)

KILLER QUEEN

Athaliah was grieved when her son Ahaziah, king of Judah, was killed. But she was not too grief-stricken to stage a coup d'ètat. She made herself the legimate ruler by murdering anyone with a claim to the throne—and that included all of Ahaziah's children. But

Ahaziah's sister got wind of her plans and sent the youngest son, Joash, into hiding. There he stayed for six years. Jehoiada, the high priest, cared for the boy until he decided the moment was right to bring down Athaliah. In a sudden, surprise public ceremony, Joash was crowned king. Jehoiada then ordered soldiers loyal to him to execute Athaliah, which they did. She was the only woman to rule over the kingdom of Judah. (See 2 Kings 11:1-15.)

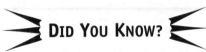

DID YOU KNOW?

Who was the goddess Asherah? What were Asherah poles? Why did the prophets of Israel passionately denounce the worship of Asherah?

Although the worship of Asherah was denounced again and again by the prophets of the Old Testament, the specific rituals associated with the worship of Asherah remain unknown to the modern Bible student. The Canaanites, a people who lived among the Israelites, revered Asherah as a goddess of fertility, perhaps even the goddess of sexuality. She was considered the wife of El, the supreme god in Canaanite mythology. The mysterious Asherah poles associated with the worship rites of this goddess were apparently tree trunks stripped of all their branches. The exact function of these poles—often associated with male and female prostitution—is unclear. What is known is that the Israelite prophets considered these poles repulsive and ordered the kings of Israel to cut them down wherever they had been placed.

STRANGE BUT TRUE

The Valley of Fire

What unspeakable crimes were committed in a ravine near Jerusalem?

Gehenna is a Hellenized form of the name for the valley of Hinnom, a ravine south of Jerusalem where deadly pagan rites were conducted. A shrine for Moabite and Ammonite gods once existed in this valley, which was the border between Judah and Benjamin. The repulsive acts conducted at this notorious site included fire-walking and the much more horrific practice of child sacrifice. The latter deed—killing the firstborn child in a fiery offering—was thought to pacify the cruel pagan deities Chemosh and Molech. Biblical archaeologists have painstakingly pieced together evidence to learn what happened in Gehenna. How did a peaceful valley so close to the religious center of Israel become the scene for some of the worst excesses of paganism? Why did so few resist deeds that were blatantly evil? How widespread was the cult? How many people lost their lives in this horrible era? Answers remain sketchy.

Gehenna's evil memory lived on in the minds of later generations. They made the word synonymous with a place of fiery torment, a prefiguring of the doctrine of hell. Eventually, King Josiah destroyed and desecrated the altars and relics of idol worship. But the prophet Jeremiah warned that in the last days, the valley of Gehenna would become a valley of slaughter, a trench in which scavengers would feed on the carcasses of countless people. This place of unspeakable evil would become a valley of judgment.

What some people do in the name of religious fervor has always baffled the modern mind. At the time, of course, those engaged in offering human sacrifices must have somehow believed their actions would appease an angry idol. But lest we get too self-righteous and look down on the primitive behavior of an ancient people, we might pause to remember that our own century also has seen its share of pointless suffering wrought by the hands of civilized peoples. Gehenna's cries of misery resonate with the agony of twentieth-century holocausts carried out in the name of righteous causes.

The story of Gehenna appears throughout the Bible. Start the tour with Joshua 15:8; 18:16; 2 Kings 23:10; 2 Chronicles 28:3; 33:6; and Jeremiah 7:31; 32:35.

SORCERERS' APPRENTICES

Scripture has always sternly warned God's people to stay away from sorcery and witchcraft. Those who practice these black arts rebel against God and place themselves and others in danger. Not surprisingly, the magicians and sorcerers we encounter in the Bible are usually up to no good. Here are three stories of sorcerers who found themselves on the wrong side of a spiritual battle.

JANNES AND JAMBRES

Magicians—even ones that worked on the wrong side—could perform astonishing feats. The sorcerers who served in Pharaoh's court knew and practiced the ways of the occult. When Aaron came before Pharaoh, he threw down his staff, which became a snake before the Pharaoh's eyes. Egypt's sorcerers were able to produce similar results, so Pharaoh remained stubbornly opposed to the warnings of Moses and Aaron. The magicians were also able to replicate some of the plagues that followed—the blood in the Nile River and the hordes of frogs that covered the landscape. They failed, however, to reproduce any of the other plagues. They seemed to recognize a force greater than they could summon. "This is the finger of God!" they exclaimed. Church tradition identifies the magicians who opposed Moses as Jannes and Jambres, and Paul refers to these men as an example of all who willfully oppose the truth. (See 2 Timothy 3:8.)

WITCH OF ENDOR

The stranger came in the cover of darkness, perhaps fearful of the consequence of his risky undertaking, for he had come to seek the counsel of a fortune-teller. Mediums had long been banned in Israel, and the penalty for practicing black arts was death. The man asked the fortune-teller, a fearful and suspicious woman, to bring up the spirit of the prophet Samuel, who had recently died. The woman screamed when she saw Samuel's ghostly form, for then she realized that her visitor was the king of Israel, Saul himself! Saul promised her that she would not be punished. Then he learned from the spirit that he would die in battle the next day and fell on the ground, overcome with fear. The prophecy proved all too true: Saul and his sons were killed by the Philistines the next day. (See 1 Samuel 28.)

ELYMAS

In the town of Paphos, Paul and Barnabas encountered a sorcerer named Bar-Jesus, also called (in Greek) Elymas. This man had become a kind of spiritual advisor to the governor of Cyprus. Fearful of losing his influence, Elymas urged the governor not to grant an audience to the missionaries. But Paul confronted Elymas for his stubborn resistance to God's ways and declared that the sorcerer would be struck with blindness. Instantly Elymas's sight failed, and he began groping in the darkness. The governor, who had witnessed this confrontation, was astonished and eagerly received Paul's words. (See Acts 13:4-12.)

◼ PORTRAITS OF SATAN

The first image of Satan most people have is of a man with horns, wearing a red suit and holding a pitchfork. That portrayal of Satan may not be completely accurate, for the Bible insists that he can change forms—even transforming himself into a beautiful angel of light. Here are some other snapshots of Satan.

1. Before his fall from heaven, Satan used to be an angel named Lucifer (Isaiah 14:12, KJV).
2. Satan wants to be God (Isaiah 14:14).
3. Satan is called the Leviathan, a swift serpent-dragon of the sea (Isaiah 27:1).
4. Before his fall, Satan was perfect in wisdom and in beauty (Ezekiel 28:12).
5. Before his fall, Satan's clothing was covered with jewels of turquoise, red carnelian, chrysolite, onyx, jasper, sapphire, beryl, white moonstone, and emerald (Ezekiel 28:13).
6. Satan, in the form of a serpent, tempted Adam and Eve (Genesis 3:1).
7. Satan appeared before God in order to get permission to destroy Job by taking away his money, family, and good health (Job 1:7–2:10).

8. Satan is the father of lies, a murderer, and a hater of truth (John 8:44).
9. Satan is called the prince of the power of the air (Ephesians 2:2).
10. Satan tries to tempt man by strategies and tricks (Ephesians 6:11).
11. Satan is called the power of darkness (Ephesians 6:12).
12. Satan is also called Beliar, meaning "vile and ruthless" (2 Corinthians 6:15).
13. Satan pretends to be an angel of light in order to deceive people (2 Corinthians 11:14).
14. Satan is called the power of death (Hebrews 2:14).
15. Satan is called the tempter (1 Thessalonians 3:5).
16. Satan wants to enslave people (2 Timothy 2:26).
17. Satan has deceived the whole world (Revelation 12:9).
18. Satan is called Apollyon, or the destroyer (Revelation 9:11).
19. Satan is depicted as a red dragon with 7 heads, 7 crowns, and 10 horns (Revelation 12:3-4).
20. Satan has a host of evil angels at his command (Revelation 12:7).
21. Jesus has defeated Satan in battle (Revelation 12:11).
22. Satan will eventually meet his doom in a lake of fire and brimstone (Revelation 20:10).

STRANGE BUT TRUE

Extraterrestrial Encounters

Who were the mysterious sons of God described in Genesis?

In a cryptic passage just before the story of Noah's ark, the writer of Genesis tells us that "sons of God" looked down on "the beautiful women of the human race" and took them as wives. Their offspring became a race of giants called the Nephilim, who became the heroes of ancient lore. (See Genesis 6:1-4.)

That is the extent of our knowledge of this moment in early

history, a puzzle that raises more questions than we have answers for. Who were these sons of God? What do we know about the Nephilim?

The least likely theory suggests that these giants were descendants of Seth, a godly line of people who had intermarried with the wicked descendants of Cain. You'll recall that Cain murdered his brother Abel; Seth was born later to Adam and Eve. Few people favor this idea anymore, though it had support in the past. The big problem: Genesis seems to draw an obvious difference between mere mortals and supermortals in this story, a difference too plain to avoid.

Another school of thought proposes that these sons of God were great men—rulers and kings. The appeal of such an explanation is that it smooths away the difficulty of imagining that angels (or some other spiritual beings) were intimate with women. Recall that great men of the Old Testament are sometimes called "sons of the Most High" and other exalted titles. But is that the author's intention? The impression we infer from the passage is that of extraordinary, supernatural beings who somehow entered earth's realm to choose earthly wives.

So that leaves us with the only other explanation—-these "sons of God" were unlike anything seen on the earth, then or now. They were from another spiritual realm—some would say a demonic one—but had certain physical capacities. They had a sex drive and their offspring were giants, powerful men—the stuff of legends. That might be too difficult to fathom: part angelic, part human beings. But whatever the Bible was speaking of in this mysterious chapter, it is clear from the books of Jude and 2 Peter that any angelic being who sins by transgressing the gulf between human and angelic will endure the full wrath of God. These angels can only expect the gloomy dungeons of God's judgment. (See 2 Peter 2:4; Jude 6.)

And what of the Nephilim? We encounter them again in Numbers 13:33, when the spies reporting from the Promised Land spoke fearfully of a race of giants that inhabited the land. Were they related to these giants of old? We can't say. But we do know that the Israelites encountered giants during their early history, Goliath of Gath being the most famous example. Second Samuel 21:15-22 includes a brief chronicle of Israel's battle with these large men.

For a firsthand account of the sons of God, read Genesis 6.

BLOOD BROTHERS

The men in these stories earned a reputation for bloodthirsty cruelty. Their life stories leave a black mark on the pages of Israel's history.

DOEG THE EDOMITE

Possibly the first hit man in the Bible, Doeg unblinkingly struck down 85 priests who had allegedly conspired with David against King Saul. The charges against these men were unjust and even ridiculous, so much so that Saul's own bodyguards refused the order to kill the priests. Saul turned to Doeg, an Edomite, who murdered the priests and then traveled to the town of Nob. There in a bloody rampage he put to death the priests' families and livestock. Only Abiathar the priest escaped to tell David about the horrendous deed. (See 1 Samuel 22.)

JOAB

David's general Joab exhibited great bravery and leadership. But he could not tolerate rivals, and he had a quick temper and an impulsive way that eventually sealed his doom. His longtime grudge against Abner, Saul's former commander who had murdered his brother Asahel, led him to kill the defenseless general in a shameful murder. He also assassinated Amasa, David's commander, with similar treachery. And against David's expressed wishes, he stabbed Absalom to death as he hung by his hair from a tree. Joab lived by the sword and died by the sword. After foolishly backing Adonijah's bid for the throne inherited by Solomon, he was executed by Benaiah while clinging to the horns of the Tabernacle altar. (See 2 Samuel 2; 1 Kings 2.)

MANASSEH

Manasseh ruled over the Northern Kingdom for over half a century, and what bleak years those must have been! He did everything in his power to undo the reforms of his godly father, Hezekiah. Besides building pagan shrines and altars, he immersed himself in the black arts of sorcery and divination. His debauchery led him to sacrifice his own son in a fiery pagan offering. The author of 2 Kings declares that "Manasseh also murdered many innocent people until Jerusalem was filled from one end to the other with innocent blood" (2 Kings 21:16). But another account in 2 Chronicles tells of a happier ending: After suffering as an Assyrian prisoner, Manasseh changed his ways and tore down the idols.

STRANGE BUT TRUE

The Queen of Heaven

What caused the prophet Jeremiah to denounce this goddess?

Who was the Queen of Heaven? Although the Bible deplores the cult that surrounded this goddess, we really know little about it. This much we know: the Queen of Heaven was widely revered in many Near Eastern societies. Sometimes she was called Ishtar, a goddess of love and fertility and identified in mythology with Venus, the brightest light in the heavens. (Some scholars feel that the worship of Ishtar prefigures the cult of the goddess Diana of Ephesus, which Paul encountered.) Prayers to the queen would secure material welfare, faithful worshipers hoped. Some of their prayers may have implored the goddess to help them with love and romantic interests. The cult had apparently flourished in Judah during the time of the prophet Jeremiah, a person who was clearly interested in neither finance nor romance.

People of all times have invented deities to meet their basic needs. Ancient people worried a lot about food, so their gods addressed those conditions beyond human control like rain, sun, pests, and sickness. Successful childbearing was crucial to the survival of any tribe. Hence, fertility gods and goddesses were fashioned as a way of coping with those needs. In many cultures, syncretism—the mixing of religious traditions—became a common practice as conquered and conqueror shared belief systems. But such practices were forbidden to Israel, which from the time of Moses had been instructed not to "make idols of any kind, whether in the shape of birds or animals or fish . . . for I, the Lord your God, am a jealous God" (Deuteronomy 5:8-9).

The worship of the Queen of Heaven symbolized the falling

darkness that would soon cover Judah. While the cult thrived, the nation was slipping into slavery at the hands of more powerful neighbors—first Egypt, then Babylon. At the time Jeremiah wrote his message, the end was near. King Jehoiakim rebelled against Babylon and for a time managed to keep the enemy at bay. His successor, Zedekiah, would not be as fortunate. During Zedekiah's reign, Nebuchadnezzar conquered and pillaged Jerusalem and sent most of its people into exile. According to Jeremiah, the worship of this mysterious goddess contributed directly to the invasion of Israel by the ferocious and bloodthirsty Babylonians.

For a glimpse of the worship of the Queen of Heaven, see Jeremiah 7:18; 44:17-19, 25.

CURIOUS CONNECTIONS

PERNICIOUS PRIESTS

Evil, corrupt, and conniving. No, these aren't descriptions of criminals, but of some of God's priests! Priests were charged with the care of the Tabernacle and with leading the people in worship. Most served honorably. But a few hardened souls surrendered their honor for power and greed. Here are the sorry tales of these renegade religious leaders.

BROTHERS GRIM

Hophni and Phinehas had everything they needed to be successful leaders. They came from a line of distinguished priests; their father, Eli, was a trusted and devout caretaker of the Tabernacle at Shiloh and a priest himself. But such heritage mattered little to these young men. They violated the rules for burnt offerings so they could have their fill of food, and they also seduced women who assisted them in front of the Tabernacle. Their continued sin brought a message of judgment from a prophet who predicted their approaching deaths. The Philistines killed Hophni and Phinehas as they carried the Ark into battle, and the family's priestly line ended. (See 1 Samuel 2:12-26; 4:10-22.)

TRAITORS, TURNCOATS, AND TREACHEROUS DUDES

Benedict Arnold was in good company with some of the people in the Bible.
Both men and women betrayed friends and their own kin for money or power.

Traitor	Action / Reference
Abner	Made an alliance with David after his king, Ishbosheth, confronted him for sleeping with his father's concubine. *2 Samuel 3:6-13*
Absalom	Led a rebellion against his father, David, but died in the struggle. *2 Samuel 15*
Achan	Jeopardized Israel's military campaign in Canaan by hoarding plunder. After a disastrous attack on Ai, Joshua discovered the crime and had Achan stoned. *Joshua 7*
Ahithophel	Counselor to King David, he sided with Absalom's bid for power. When Absalom later rejected his advice, he committed suicide. *2 Samuel 17:23*
David	Betrayed Uriah by sleeping with his wife, then compounded the crime by having Uriah sent to his death in battle. *2 Samuel 11*
Delilah	Cooperated with the Philistines to betray Samson. She eventually coaxed the secret of Samson's strength out of him. This led to his capture. *Judges 16*
Jacob	Betrayed his twin brother Esau's trust and his father's intentions by pretending to be Esau. He received his brother's birthright but had to flee for his life. *Genesis 27*
Jezebel	Had some rogues proclaim that Naboth was a traitor to God and the king, so Naboth was stoned to death. Her husband, King Ahab, then took Naboth's vineyard, which he had coveted. *1 Kings 21*
Joseph's brothers: sons of Jacob	Sick of their brother's special place with their father, nine brothers plotted to kill Joseph. They settled for selling him to Midianite slave traders for 20 pieces of silver. *Genesis 37:17-36*
Judas	Betrayed Jesus to the Pharisees for 30 pieces of silver. His kiss was the signal for Jesus' arrest. *Matthew 26:14-16, 47-50; Mark 14:10-11, 43-50; Luke 22:47; John 18:1-6*

Miriam and Aaron	Out of jealousy, they challenged Moses' authority. This act of rebellion caused Miriam to suffer a short bout of leprosy. *Numbers 12*
Peter	Pretended not to know Jesus when Jesus was suffering through his trial before the Pharisees. Jesus had predicted his denial. *Mark 14:66-72; John 18:15-18, 25-27*
Shimei	Cursed David when David was forced to flee from Absalom's invading army. *1 Samuel 16:5-13*
Zimri	Killed Baasha, king of Israel, then assumed power. When the army heard of Baasha's death, they chose a new king and turned on Zimri. After a seven-day reign, Zimri killed himself after the army took the capital of Tirzah. *1 Kings 16:8-20*

I DON'T WANT TO HEAR IT

The prophet Jeremiah drew enemies as if he were a magnet. His habit of blunt talk and fearless preaching to the rich and powerful made many a hearer uncomfortable. One day Jeremiah stopped outside the Temple and proclaimed a message of doom to those present. Pashur, the priest in charge of the Temple, heard Jeremiah and had him arrested. Pashur added to Jeremiah's humiliation by having him flogged and put in stocks. When Jeremiah was released the next day, he told Pashur that he and his entourage would be sent into exile for their refusal to heed the prophet's warnings. (See Jeremiah 20.)

THE HIGH PRIEST BEFORE THE HIGH PRIEST

In Hebrews 7, Jesus is described as a great high priest who intercedes for sinners in God's presence. How ironic, then, that Jesus was condemned to death by an unworthy high priest, Caiaphas. Matthew tells us that Caiaphas presided over the farce trial that brought forth several false witnesses to accuse Jesus of wrongdoing. His melodramatic reaction to Jesus' alleged blasphemy led the religious leaders to vote for death. Later he orchestrated the events that convinced Pontius Pilate to release Barabbas and carry out Jesus' sentence as the priests demanded. (See Matthew 26:1–27:22.)

THE WHITEWASHED WALL

"Brothers, I have always lived before God in all good conscience!" With those words Paul began his address to the High Council. But he didn't see the punch coming. Ananias, the high priest who heard those words, ordered the men standing next to Paul to slap him on the mouth. Infuriated by such ill treatment—after all, he had not even been charged with a crime—Paul retorted, "God will slap you, you whitewashed wall!" But after learning that Ananias was the high priest, Paul offered a quick apology. Ironically, Paul's heated remark proved to be prophetic. Ananias, widely despised by Jews for his corruption and favoritism toward Rome, was later hunted down and murdered by his own people. (See Acts 23:1-5.)

STRANGE BUT TRUE

The Mysterious Death of Judas Iscariot

How did Jesus' betrayer end his days?

The name Judas Iscariot will forever be linked with treachery and betrayal. Like Benedict Arnold's treason, Judas Iscariot's selfish deed earns him a place with the most notorious turncoats who ever lived. But the circumstances of his death have always puzzled scholars. The Gospel of Matthew stipulates that Judas hanged himself, but the book of Acts suggests that he plunged to his death. Which is correct?

Jesus himself chose Judas to be one of his 12 disciples, the close circle of men who traveled with Jesus and were taught by him. Yet Judas's three years of seeing the miracles and ministry of Jesus did little to change his heart. Jesus verbalized this at one point, telling his disciples that "one [of you] is a devil" (John 6:70). The Bible does not suggest why Judas wanted to betray Jesus, saying only that "Satan entered into Judas Iscariot" (Luke 22:3). Whatever the reason, Judas conspired with the religious leaders who were looking for allies in their plot against Jesus. In exchange for 30 pieces of silver, Judas agreed to lure Jesus to a place where the authorities could easily arrest him.

After Jesus was bound and sentenced to death, Judas seems to have had an attack of conscience. He returned the money to the chief priests and elders and said, "I have sinned, for I have betrayed an innocent man" (Matthew 27:4). The religious leaders were unmoved. Having achieved their goal, they had no concern that Judas was remorseful. In a final act of frustration, Judas threw the money into the Temple and left.

What he did next remains a mystery. Matthew says, "[He] went out and hanged himself" (27:5). The book of Acts, however, provides a more gruesome and, some say, contradictory description of Judas's demise: "Falling there, he burst open, spilling out his intestines" (1:18).

So which is it? Did Judas hang himself or did he leap to his death?

Actually, these two seemingly disparate descriptions can be fit together logically. One possibility is that after Judas hanged himself, his body was not discovered for some time. Therefore, when his body finally fell, either because of decay or because someone cut it down, it was so decomposed that it burst open. Another possibility is that the word *hanged* in Matthew actually means "impaled." If Judas chose to impale himself, as it were, on the rocks below, it would certainly explain the gruesome condition of the body described in Acts. Yet another explanation suggests that Judas strangled himself on a tree. As he lost consciousness, his body dropped and split open on the rocks below.

For more information, see Matthew 27 and Acts 1.

HISTORY'S GREATEST VILLAIN

Who is the Antichrist? For centuries, men and women have speculated on the identity of this incarnation of evil who will bring about the last battle between good and evil. The word Antichrist *itself appears only in 1 and 2 John. It can refer to anyone who opposes the work of Christ, but other Scripture references suggest also that there will be an Antichrist—a world leader who will incarnate all that is wicked. The following list includes some of the identifying characteristics of the Antichrist.*

Characteristics of the Antichrist / Reference

He will be a ruler whose sudden rise will astonish everyone, and he will dominate a powerful group of ten allies who will rule the world. *Daniel 7:7-12*

As ruthless as the ten-horned beast proves to be, the Antichrist—the dominant horn—will be more bloodthirsty still, persecuting God's people and defying God. *Daniel 7:21*

Jerusalem will again be destroyed, and a treaty will be established for seven years between Israel and the forces of the Antichrist. *Daniel 9:27*

The Antichrist will exalt himself with a religious fervor. *Daniel 11:36-39*

The Antichrist will wage war in the Middle East. *Daniel 11:40-43; Joel 3:19*

The Antichrist will make claims to be a messiah or savior. Many will follow. *Matthew 24:5*

The Antichrist will have such disregard for righteousness that Paul calls him "the man of lawlessness." He will perform signs and counterfeit miracles. To crown his arrogance, he will occupy God's Temple and publicly proclaim himself to be divine. *2 Thessalonians 2:3-4*

The rule of the Antichrist will be marked by evil teaching and shameful immorality. *2 Peter 2:1-2*

The life of the Antichrist will stand out by its degree of evil. *2 Thessalonians 2:9-10*

The Antichrist will add his powerful voice to the chorus of those who deny that Jesus is the Son of God. *1 John 2:22; see also 1 John 4:3*

The Antichrist will make a case against the historicity and humanity of Jesus. *2 John 1:7*

The Antichrist will oppose and murder two outspoken witnesses for Christ, whose bodies will lie exposed in Jerusalem. Three and a half days later they will be raised to life and taken by God in plain sight of all. *Revelation 11:7-12*

The Antichrist will attempt to gain control over the necessities of food and essential services. He will enforce the worship of evil. *Revelation 13:11-18*

LIARS' CLUB

"Do not testify falsely against your neighbor," proclaims the ninth commandment. But some people never learn. These liars told some whoppers to improve their standing or to cover up embarrassment. But as they discovered, the truth always wins out!

ZIBA

Ziba profited greatly from the kindness of King David, but he wanted more. He was the servant of Saul and became the overseer of the lands given by David to Mephibosheth, Saul's grandson. When Absalom rebelled against his father, Ziba sided with David but claimed that Mephibosheth had welcomed the uprising as a chance to reclaim the throne for his family. Upon hearing that, David gave all Mephibosheth's land to Ziba. David confronted Mephibosheth after he returned to Jerusalem, only to hear a different story: Mephibosheth had wanted to accompany the king, but Ziba had prevented him. His humble actions told David plainly that Ziba had lied; but put in a difficult spot, David chose a weak compromise: he divided the land between the two men. (See 2 Samuel 16:1-4; 19:24-30.)

HANANIAH

Like it or not, prophets often had to deliver news that was gloomy or highly critical of the status quo. Jeremiah fell into that category. His messages brought him complaints, persecution, and imprisonment. No wonder the public embraced the glad tidings of Hananiah, another prophet, who promised Judah that its slavery to Babylon would soon be over. In a public confrontation with Jeremiah, Hananiah smashed to bits the yoke Jeremiah was wearing and predicted the release of Israel's captives. Encouraging as that news was, Hananiah's words were false. Jeremiah returned to announce that Judah's destruction was imminent—and that Hananiah would die soon. Two months later, the false prophet died, and within a few years Jerusalem lay in ruins. (See Jeremiah 28:1-17.)

THE ROMAN GUARDS

The embarrassment and shame must have crushed the proud soldiers. They had been sent to guard the tomb of Jesus at the request of the Pharisees, to keep the disciples from stealing the body. At dawn they awoke to an earthquake and the presence of an angel. They fell into a dead faint, and when they recovered, the tomb was empty! Hurriedly they met with the religious leaders, who helped them devise the only excuse anyone might believe—that the disciples had indeed stolen the body. The guards were no doubt grateful for the leaders' cooperation, for such seeming ineptitude on their part could have resulted in their execution. Matthew remarks that the religious leaders eagerly spread the tale and that many continued to believe it years later. (See Matthew 27:62–28:15.)

STRANGE BUT TRUE

Babylon, Then and Now

What happened to the great international hub of world power and commerce?

It was one of the greatest cities of the ancient world, the capital of Mesopotamia, southwest of modern Baghdad. But it became a symbol of satanic deception and worldly power, the "kingdom of the beast."

Babylon's origin will likely remain a mystery, but its rise to power begins to appear in recorded history around the time of the great Hammurabi, the best-known king of the Third Dynasty of ancient Ur. The Hittites occupied it next, then the Assyrians. The brutal Assyrian king Sennacherib destroyed the city in 689 B.C., but his obstinate son rebuilt it. It begins to figure prominently in Bible history around the time of Nebuchadnezzar (605–562 B.C.) and later during the rule of the Persian King Cyrus.

Babylon's greatness began to wane after Nebuchadnezzar's death. After a series of ineffective kings, Babylon was occupied by the Medes and Persians. Decades later, Alexander the Great built

Seleucia nearby, and the city slipped into obscurity. By A.D. 200, Babylon was largely a ghost town.

So what is Babylon today?

Once the seat of wealth and lavish splendor, Babylon is now a mound of dirt, a place where archaeologists gather to salvage what they can, given the region's high water table. It is a ruin, a Tel, or a pile of junk, depending on your professional point of view. But its meaning in the Bible continues to tell the sad story of this city's relentless wickedness: When the New Testament writers try to describe the despicable mess the world will find itself in just before the return of Jesus Christ, they use Babylon, a city of corruption, treachery, and murder, as an example. Few ancient cities have had such a blackened reputation or been associated with corruption and evil as Babylon has.

For more on Babylon, read Jeremiah 25, the book of Daniel, and Revelation 18.

CURIOUS CONNECTIONS

CHURCH CREEPS

The world is full of impostors, swindlers, and charlatans—those creeps your mother warned you about long ago. They lurk everywhere—including in churches, unfortunately. The New Testament mentions the disgraceful deeds of a few infamous characters who spread dissension, told lies, and in general set a bad example. Here are their stories.

SIMON THE SORCERER

Simon Magus knew that the new faith he had witnessed was powerful—more powerful that any he had ever seen. He was also one of the first to recognize that this power could make him wealthy. Before he joined the church, Simon had been a magician. His tricks would not only amaze onlookers but would also motivate gullible people to dig deep into their purses. Simon became envious of Peter's supernatural gifts of healing, so he offered Peter money to learn how to give people the Holy Spirit by laying his hands on them. Peter responded with a sharp rebuke. In fear, Simon repented of his greed and begged for forgiveness. But was

MURDERERS' ROW: KILLERS IN THE BIBLE

The Bible does not shrink from recording the sordid details of perverse and wicked people—from gory murders to persistent family jealousies. The Bible reader finds a whole list of real-life people with real-life problems. Just as modern society has its murderers, so did ancient Israel. Here is murderers' row.

Murderer	Circumstance	Result	Reference
Cain	Out of jealousy, killed his brother Abel	Became a fugitive who wandered the earth	*Genesis 4:1-16*
Lamech	Killed a youth who supposedly tried to harm him	Challenged any who dared to avenge the death	*Genesis 4:23*
Simeon and Levi	Killed the entire population of Shechem to avenge their sister's rape	Jacob feared he would be despised by the Perizzites and Canaanites.	*Genesis 34:1-31*
Moses	Killed an Egyptian taskmaster	Fled to the desert of Midian, where he stayed for many years	*Exodus 2:11-12*
Ehud	Assassinated Eglon, king of Moab	Israel defeated Moab and lived in peace for 80 years.	*Judges 3:12-30*
Jael	Struck down Sisera, Canaanite army commander	Fulfilled message of the prophetess Deborah	*Judges 4:1-21*
Abimelech	Slew his 70 half brothers	Killed himself during the siege of Thebez	*Judges 9:5*
Gibeonites	Murdered Levite's concubine	Sparked a civil war with the rest of Israel	*Judges 19*

Name	Deed	Result	Reference
Doeg	Murdered 85 priests of Nob	Confirmed Saul's deterioration and David's favor with God	1 Samuel 22:18
Unnamed Amalekite	Hoping to earn David's favor, he claimed to have killed Saul.	David ordered his execution for killing the Lord's anointed king.	2 Samuel 1:10-16
Joab	Murdered Abner in retaliation for his brother Asahel's death	Joab became unquestioned commander of David's army.	2 Samuel 3:22-39
Baanah and Recab	Beheaded Ishbosheth as a prize for David	David condemned their murder of an innocent man and had them executed.	2 Samuel 4:1-12
Absalom	Ordered the murder of Amnon for raping his sister Tamar	Absalom was estranged from David for many years, but they were reconciled for a short time.	2 Samuel 13:29
Joab	Killed Absalom as he dangled from a tree	Joab earned David's displeasure and was demoted.	2 Samuel 18:1-18
Joab	Treacherously struck down Amasa, David's general	Joab's bloody deeds would result in his own death (2 Kings 2).	2 Samuel 20:10
Baasha	Killed Nadab, king of Israel	Became king, but his evil deeds brought judgment	1 Kings 15:28-29
Zimri	Killed Elah, son of Baasha	Ruled as king for a week, then committed suicide	1 Kings 16:8-10
Jezebel	Conspired to have Naboth stoned to death	Jehu would have her killed for her crimes.	1 Kings 21:11-16
Hazael	Suffocated Ben-hadad, king of Aram	Became king and oppressor of Israel	2 Kings 8:7-15

Name	Deed	Result	Reference
Athaliah	Murdered the children of her dead son, Ahaziah, so she could rule in his place	The priest Jehoiada hid Ahaziah's son Joash and revolted against her six years later.	2 Kings 11:1
Jozacar and Jehozabad	Trusted advisors, they assassinated their king Joash.	Amaziah became king of Judah.	2 Kings 12:20-21
Menahem	Killed Shallum, king of Israel	Became king, but his reign was over shadowed by an Assyrian invasion	2 Kings 15:13-14
Pekah	Assassinated Pekahiah, king of Israel	Became king but was himself assassinated	2 Kings 15:25
Hoshea	Killed Pekah, king of Israel	Became king but was soon imprisoned by the Assyrians	2 Kings 15:30
Adrammelech and Sharezer	Murdered their father Sennacherib, king of Assyria	Their brother, Esarhaddon, became king.	2 Kings 19:37
Ishmael	Killed Gedaliah, puppet ruler of Judah appointed by Nebuchadnezzar	Babylon exacted retribution, and Judeans fled.	2 Kings 25:22-26
Herod	Murdered the infants of Judea	His attempt to kill Jesus failed.	Matthew 2:13-18
Barabbas	Arrested for murder during an insurrection	Released during Passover instead of Jesus	Luke 23:19
Herod Agrippa I	Put James to death	Soon died of a sudden illness	Acts 12:1-2

it a genuine change of heart? Church fathers writing in the first and second centuries frequently speak of a group of heretics called Simonians, a group that took its name from Simon. Scholars, however, debate whether this group was actually connected with the Simon of the Bible. We can say with certainty that Simon's story contributed a word to our English language—*simony,* the deplorable practice of buying or selling a church office. (See Acts 8:9-25.)

THE CARNAL CORINTHIAN

Hostility and indifference are what most people expect from enemies but not from their friends, neighbors, or fellow church members. Sadly, the apostle Paul endured all sorts of ill treatment from the Corinthian church. One man, in particular, had divided the assembly with his controversial deeds. Paul does not mention his name or specify what he did. However, it is clear that Paul wrote a strong letter to the Corinthians urging them to discipline the offender. Some Bible scholars identify the troublemaker with the man who had shamelessly slept with the wife of his own father, an act that Paul sternly condemned in his first letter to the Corinthians. But most scholars believe the offender was yet another agitator in the controversy-stricken Corinthian church. Paul's letter apparently had a great effect, because in his second letter to the Corinthians, he implores the church to reconcile with the man, who had come to recognize his error. (See 2 Corinthians 2:5-8.)

DIOTREPHES THE DICTATOR

Churches typically bring out the more charitable, caring, and generous side of people. But some people are incurably power-hungry— even in a house of worship. Diotrephes was one such character. Diotrephes' desire for complete authority brought him into conflict with the apostle John. His tool for controlling others was ostracism. Any member of his church who housed a traveling missionary or a messenger from John faced expulsion. Diotrephes thought it better to see a missionary sleep on the streets than to allow another person to influence his flock. To further insulate his followers, he spread rumors, malicious gossip, and outright lies about outsiders. John urged his fellow Christians not to be influenced by this "bad example" and promised to report Diotrephes' behavior to church authorities. (See 3 John 1.)

DID YOU KNOW?

Why would the Hebrews worship a calf? How could a golden statue inspire an orgy?

The story of the golden calf still evokes surprise in modern readers. Why would people want to worship an object they had made with their own hands? And how could they forget the law Moses had presented to them just days before? The first commandment, above all, warned the Israelites not to worship false gods. But Aaron, Moses' brother and future high priest, yielded to popular pressure and made a calf out of gold. The people responded with an unrestrained orgy of drinking and carousing.

Scholars have debated the appeal of this idol for centuries. Some have suggested that it wasn't actually a calf, but a bull. The writers of the Bible used the word *calf* to express their contempt for the object the Israelites worshiped. The bull was worshiped by many in the ancient Middle East. For instance, the Egyptians worshiped Hapi, a god represented by a bull. But most scholars believe that the Israelites were modeling their "calf" on the bulls that embodied the Canaanite god Baal. In ancient times, a bull was a common symbol of fertility. This could explain why a calf might spark all kinds of debauchery.

 FAQs (frequently asked questions)

DEMONS AND DEMON POSSESSION

Isn't believing in demons superstitious?

Certainly the writers of the Bible took demons seriously. Jesus, the disciples, and the early Christians confronted them frequently and warned other believers about their power to resist God's work. The demon activities described in the Bible cannot be explained away as mere physical or emotional illnesses (see, for instance, Mark 5:1-13). Moreover, there are many well-documented cases of supernatural activity in many cultures today that bear a striking similarity to the demonic accounts in the New Testament.

Where did demons come from?
The Bible does not say for sure. The presence of evil, however, is evident from the beginning of creation, when the serpent tempted Eve (Genesis 3:1-5). The prophet Isaiah describes a being ("son of Dawn") whose pride and lust for power caused him to challenge the Most High (Isaiah 14:12). His rebellion caused him to be hurled to the pit ("Sheol"). Some scholars have suggested that the son of Dawn was, in fact, Satan and that demons were angels who followed his rebellion and were banned from God's presence. In Mark 3:22, Satan is called the prince of demons.

Are demons active in the world today?
One of the most popular and imaginative works of C. S. Lewis, *The Screwtape Letters,* works from the assumption that demons are indeed active in our world. But how can we see the evidence? Scripture describes several signs of demonic work, including human possession, occult ritual and sacrifice, supernatural disturbances, and deceitful teachings. Demons may also resist the work of God's angels.

What will happen to demons at the end of the world?
Jesus said they would be thrown into an eternal fire (Matthew 25:41). John's vision described in the book of Revelation uses vivid language to depict Satan's doom: Satan will be hurled into the Lake of Fire and burned day and night without end. (See Revelation 20:10.)

Why wouldn't Jesus let demons talk?
Two basic explanations have been offered. First, Jesus did not want the crowds to think of him as a wonder-worker and sensationalist; the encounters with the demons, who often shrieked and shouted in his presence, could have distracted Jesus' audience from his teaching. Second, Jesus clearly wanted to reveal his identity and mission according to God's timetable, not

Satan's. To disclose that news too soon may have encouraged the wrong expectations—namely, that his ministry of healing was more important than his work of salvation. (See Mark 1:21-27.)

How does a person become possessed?

In the book of Acts we find an account of demon possession that was linked to fortune-telling, an activity strictly forbidden by Old Testament law. Paul also speaks of the "sacrifices . . . offered to demons" (1 Corinthians 10:20). Both cases suggest that possession may occur from involvement in a cult or occult activities, including sacrifices and spiritualism, or through prolonged exposure to harmful, self-destructive habits. Those who have studied contemporary instances of demon possession affirm this idea. (Interestingly, many of the cases of demon possession in the New Testament happen in areas where pagan worship and Jewish practice overlapped.)

Can demons read our minds?

We can't say with certainty. We can say that demons are shrewd and know the vulnerable points of human behavior. In his letter to the Ephesians, Paul urges Christians to put on spiritual armor to resist the attacks of the devil. "For we are not fighting against people made of flesh and blood, but against the evil rulers and authorities of the unseen world, against those mighty powers of darkness who rule this world, and against wicked spirits in the heavenly realms" (Ephesians 6:12). It seems logical to conclude that such spiritual warfare is fought in human hearts and minds. Those who take faith as their shield (Ephesians 6:16) will be able to ward off the fiery darts of Satan.

Do exorcisms really happen today?

Fortunately, cases of demon possession are relatively rare. Yet many Christian denominations recognize that demonic activity is real and sometimes rely on skilled spiritual experts to confront and expel demons. Exorcisms (also called services of deliverance) clearly require discernment and must be performed with great caution. We find in the New Testament at least two incidents of exorcisms that failed because of disbelief or lack of spiritual understanding. (See Matthew 17:14-18; Acts 19:13-16.)

FOUR

ENIGMATIC EVENTS

Dangerous Escapes and Mighty Warriors

The Lost Ark

What happened to Israel's most holy object?

In 1981, *Raiders of the Lost Ark* took movie viewers by storm. The plot related the adventures of an inquisitive archaeologist who wrests the Ark of the Covenant from the evil intentions of the Nazis, only to lose it again. Though entirely fictitious, *Raiders* revived interest in one of the most puzzling mysteries of the last 2,000 years: namely, what happened to Israel's most holy object?

It is amazing that a simple box of acacia wood 4 by 2 by 2 feet could inspire so much fear and reverence. That box is, of course, the Ark of the Covenant—the box that occupied the Most Holy Place, the inner sanctuary of the Temple of God. Built when the Israelites were still nomads in the wilderness, the Ark of the Covenant was the centerpiece of Israel's worship. In it were stored the two tablets of the Decalogue (the Ten Commandments), a bowl of manna (the food during Israel's long march to the Promised Land), and Aaron's rod (which facilitated the miracles in Egypt that led to the Exodus). For many years it stayed in the Tabernacle, a large tent that traveled with the Israelites. Later Solomon placed the Ark in the magnificent Temple he built, and it rested in a chamber known as the Holy of Holies.

The precise time when the Ark of the Covenant was lost remains an intriguing mystery. Many believe that the Babylonians destroyed it when they sacked Jerusalem in 586 B.C. Others say that Shishak of Egypt destroyed it when he plundered the Temple. But others say that the Ark was taken and hidden somewhere else and still exists at some unknown location even today.

One theory is that Shishak stole the Ark and took it to Egypt. This idea emerges strongly in the film *Raiders of the Lost Ark*. Unfortunately, there is no evidence or even legend to support this theory.

Others believe that the Ark is somewhere closer to Jerusalem. Some suggested sites include Mount Nebo in Jordan and the region of Qumran, where the Dead Sea Scrolls were found. But again, there is no evidence that the Ark was ever taken to either site.

Still others say that the Ark is actually in Jerusalem, buried in a cave or under the stones of the old city. A group of ultra-orthodox Jews believe that the Ark is under the Temple mount. Others say it is in a tunnel under the city streets.

Perhaps most intriguing of all is the theory that the Ark was taken to Ethiopia in the days of Solomon. This view has been made popular by the recent book *The Sign and the Seal: The Quest for the Lost Ark of the Covenant* by Graham Hancock. This theory is based on Ethiopian folklore that Solomon fathered a child by the queen of Sheba. Ethiopia is one possible location of the land of Sheba. The legends say that this son, named Menelik, whisked the Ark away to Ethiopia for safekeeping. But as with all the other theories, no one has seen the Ark or produced any evidence beyond the folklore that it is safely tucked away in northern Africa.

Whatever the case, the Ark has been lost. The Second Temple, erected under Ezra and Nehemiah, contained no replacement or facsimile of the Ark. There was truly only one of its kind, and it could not be replaced.

Could the Ark have survived? Might it still be found somewhere in the desert sands of the Middle East?

If you travel near Axum in northern Ethiopia, you will hear that the Ark is kept under lock and key and out of sight in the Maryam Tsion Church. That is the lore among the people of that region. No other place or people claim to know its whereabouts.

To learn about the Ark for yourself, read Exodus 25; Joshua 3;
1 Samuel 4; and 1 Chronicles 13.

STRANGE BUT TRUE

Dinner Bell at the Lion Pit

How did a prophet withstand the appetites of wild beasts?

One of the world's most famous restaurants is The Carnivore in Nairobi, Kenya. There patrons enjoy an unusual buffet of zebra, python, wildebeest, warthog, goat, and gazelle, but the most coveted dish is lion. Perhaps because a hungry lion is indeed "king of the jungle," the offer of lion on a menu seems like such an odd reversal of nature: the "man-eater" grilled to order.

Daniel, under the rule of Darius the Mede, conqueror of Babylon, was himself served up to lions in a cruel reversal of The Carnivore's cuisine. Laws at the time forbade prayers to anyone but Darius himself. For praying to God, Daniel was to be food for hungry beasts in the king's special execution pits.

Whether Daniel was afraid, worried, nervous, or upset, we don't know. However, we do know that Daniel was a determined man. He wouldn't bow to just any wish—even if it came from the emperor himself. Daniel kept praying to the God of Israel, the God he believed in. He stood up for his convictions and would not redirect his prayers to a person he knew was as mortal as he.

So Daniel was sentenced to the lion pit, and the sentence was carried out. But the lions did not disturb Daniel. Although he sat right beside them, they didn't touch him. The lions' dinner, Daniel himself, walked out of the pit the next morning, alive and well. Why would lions suddenly go on a hunger strike?

Lions eat only when hungry, not for recreation. Perhaps Daniel was fortunate to arrive during one of their siestas when they were not hungry. But the whole point of having a bunch of lions caged up was to keep them hungry. The ancients would typically starve lions so they could watch the ferocious lions tear up the ones convicted.

The fact that these lions were starving is proven by how they savagely tore apart Daniel's false accusers. These were hungry lions.

Then what kept these lions from devouring Daniel? It remains a mystery how Daniel survived a night trapped in a pit filled with hungry lions. Perhaps some strange and quiet influence sedated their wild instincts for just a night—the night of Daniel's sojourn. Daniel himself put it more directly: "My God sent his angel to shut the lions' mouths so that they would not hurt me, for I have been found innocent in his sight" (Daniel 6:22).

Daniel lived for quite a few more years and never stopped praying to his God.

For more on Daniel among the lions, read Daniel 6.

CURIOUS CONNECTIONS

LEFT STANDING AT THE ALTAR
The altar has been the cornerstone of worship for many civilizations. In ancient Israel, the altar received gifts of thanksgiving and offerings of atonement for sin. Even at these holy places, however, the unexpected could suddenly occur. . . .

A DREADED SACRIFICE
Isaac was the son God had promised Abraham. According to the Lord, he was going to make a great nation from Abraham's descendants. So it must have seemed odd to Abraham when God commanded him to build an altar and offer Isaac as a sacrifice. Without even a hint of objection, Abraham obeyed. After preparing the necessary wood, Abraham tied up his son and placed him on the altar. Surprisingly, Isaac did not resist. As Abraham raised his knife to kill his son, an angel of the Lord stopped him. God was so pleased by Abraham's obedience that he provided a ram to complete the interrupted sacrifice. Abraham's descendants—by way of his son Isaac—became the Jewish nation. (See Genesis 22:1-19.)

ARK OF THE COVENANT LINKED TO MYSTERIOUS DEATHS

Case	Circumstance	Result
Eli and his family *1 Samuel 4:4-22*	Eli, judge and priest, fails to stop the detestable behavior of his sons, Hophni and Phinehas. Both young men are priests but use their position to extort bribes and favors.	A series of disasters follows, each related in some way to the Ark, each resulting in death. Hophni and Phinehas carry the Ark into battle, thinking it will protect them. Instead, both die at the hands of the Philistines, and the Ark is captured. When Eli hears that the Ark has been taken, he falls from his chair and breaks his neck. His daughter-in-law goes into labor after hearing that the Ark has been captured and dies shortly thereafter.
The Philistines *1 Samuel 5:1-12*	Having captured the Ark, the Philistines celebrate their victory and put the Ark in a shrine to their god Dagon.	The triumph dissolves into terror after a plague breaks out. The pestilence becomes so widespread that the Ark is moved to two other cities, with the same results: "Those who don't die are afflicted with tumors; and there is weeping everywhere" (1 Samuel 5:12). So anxious are the Philistines to end the plague that they place the Ark on an oxcart, believing that the God of Israel will guide the animals to the town of Beth-shemesh in Israel. The Lord leads the animals straight to the town.
70 men of Beth-shemesh *1 Samuel 6:19-20*	The people of Beth-shemesh rejoice that the Ark is in Israel's possession again. But 70 curiosity seekers make the mistake of looking into the Ark.	The men of Beth-shemesh certainly would have known about the penalty for looking on the holiness of God (Numbers 4:20); no person could see God and live. Consequently, all 70 die.
Uzzah *2 Samuel 6:6-7*	King David is moving the Ark to Jerusalem using an oxcart. During the journey, the oxen stumble, and a man named Uzzah reaches out to steady the Ark.	Uzzah ignores clear warnings about touching the Ark. It is a holy dwelling place for God and cannot be touched by human hands. Uzzah dies instantly.

THE VOW

Jephthah was chosen by the people of his region to lead Israel in battle against the Ammonites. Before going to war, Jephthah made a rash vow to the Lord. Jephthah swore that if the Lord delivered the Ammonites into his hands, he would offer as a sacrifice the first thing that ran out of his house to greet him when he returned. You can probably guess what happened next: God delivered the Ammonites into Jephthah's hands. When the warrior returned home triumphantly, his daughter rushed out of his house to greet him. In order to fulfill his vow to the Lord, Jephthah had to offer his own daughter as a sacrifice. (See Judges 11.)

YOU CAN'T DO THAT!

The building of an altar once nearly ignited a civil war among the tribes of Israel. The tribes that had settled on the east side of the Jordan—Reuben, Gad, and the half-tribe of Manasseh—had built an altar as a memorial. But the other tribes, fearful that the easterners had plunged into idolatry, prepared for war to purge idolatry from their people. At a formal summit, the eastern tribes argued persuasively that they had not intended to rebel, only to remind their descendants that they too were people of the living God. Their words won the day, and bloodshed was averted. The people of Gad and Reuben then named their altar Witness to show their unity with all Israel. (See Joshua 22:10-34.)

BAAL BUSTER

Gideon, one of Israel's most famous judges, took a hard line against idolatry. The Lord had instructed him to tear down his father's altar to Baal and cut down the Asherah pole beside it. He was then to build an altar to the Lord using the wood of the pole to make the sacrifice. Gideon did exactly as he was told, but the town was outraged by Gideon's deed. They demanded that Gideon's father hand over his son to be executed, but his father refused and challenged Baal to defend himself. From that moment on, Gideon was known as Jerub-baal, which means "Let Baal defend himself." (See Judges 6:24-32.)

THE LONG AND AMAZING LIFE OF THE BIBLE

The Bible is one of the oldest books known to humankind. So venerated were the scrolls of God's word that some Jewish rabbis taught that those who were going to touch the Scriptures would have to wash their hands, carefully and reverently. Moreover, the Jewish scribes who copied the Scriptures were even more meticulous. One error would mean throwing away the entire scroll. Just the fact that this book has survived the test of time is amazing. Below is a list of the twists and turns of the long history of this manuscript.

What Happened?	When?
It's been broken.	When Moses returned the first time from Mount Sinai with the stone tablets upon which God had engraved the Law, he discovered the people in a pagan orgy. In anger, he threw down the tablets and broke them. After Moses' punishment and repentance, God issued a "second printing" of the Law. *Exodus 32:19-20; 34:1-35*
It's been boxed and engraved.	Efforts to apply the commands in Deuteronomy 6:8-9 resulted in several traditions that still characterize the Jewish people. The phrase "tie them to your hands as a reminder, and wear them on your forehead" developed into the "tefillin," which are black straps with small boxes attached to the end. Devout Jewish males wear two of these tefillin in worship—one wrapped around their head so the box containing handwritten Scripture hangs between their eyes, and the other wrapped around an arm.
It's been praised.	The phrase "write them on the doorposts of your house" led to the creation of "mezuzahs," hollow plaques that are nailed to the door frames in homes and include inside a tiny scroll of Deuteronomy 6:4.

It's been lost and found.	A talented worshiper wrote an encyclopedic psalm in which every one of 176 verses expresses respect and honor for God's word—Psalm 119. During Josiah's reign, the Temple in Jerusalem was cleaned out and restored. As debris was removed, a scroll-copy of the Law was discovered. Apparently, neglect had resulted in the loss or misplacing of the Scriptures. The warnings and promised judgments added fuel to a spiritual revival in the land. *2 Kings 22:8-13*
It's been cut and burned.	King Jehoiakim sliced off sections of Jeremiah's scroll and burned them after hearing what God had instructed the prophet to write. *Jeremiah 36:21-25*
It's been eaten.	After singling out the prophet Ezekiel for special service, God included in Ezekiel's vision a scroll that he had the prophet eat. Although the writings on the scroll were full of sorrow, Ezekiel reported that the taste of the scroll was sweet. *Ezekiel 2:9–3:3*
It's been twisted.	Jesus pointed out with anger that some "applications" of Scripture actually resulted in twisting God's commands. For example, teachers in Jesus' day told people that the necessity for caring for their parents could be avoided if they merely "dedicated" all their belongings to God. *Mark 7:6-13*

The Best for Last

What explains the unexpected presence of wine at a wedding?

Sparkling red wine—at first glance, nothing seems peculiar, intriguing, or mysterious about a simple glass of wine. The natural processes of fermentation are widely known. Even a small child knows when the milk has been too long in the refrigerator. But one hot day in the little dusty town of Cana, simple jars of wine were not only the source of merriment but the source of wonder and bewilderment. What exactly was the mysterious drink that poured out of those stone jars?

Throughout the day, no one had suspected anything. It was a normal wedding. The merry guests had gathered. But it seems that before the party had run its course, the wine had run out—a serious social blunder. Jesus and his mother were present. With a maternal concern for the host, she prompted Jesus to do something. What could Jesus do? Why would his mother ask him for help?

After protesting to his mother that his "time has not yet come"— a mysterious statement in itself—Jesus calmly told the house servants to fill six stone jars with fresh, cool water. By the time the servants brought a cup of water from these stone jars to the host, the liquid had mysteriously changed its molecular structure so that it was sparkling wine, the best the master of the banquet had ever tasted.

How did this occur? It is clear that we must dismiss notions of stretching a little leftover wine with water to appease the guests. Ordinarily, the last wine bottle to be served was the newest wine and thus the least tasty. Diluting it would be pointless. Somehow the distillation process went into rapid overdrive and produced, almost instantaneously, what normally takes years. How did Jesus do that?

Well, maybe he didn't. Maybe the wine he made was really a grape juice that seemed to the already merry crowd like one of the cellar's best, but without the intoxicating quality.

Then again, maybe he did. The guests reported that Jesus had produced the very best wine. At face value, that eliminates the grape juice explanation. These ancient wine connoisseurs would not rave about juice that didn't sparkle. This was choice wine, a delight to the host and his company.

How could water—not even grape juice—turn into wine within minutes? Some would say it is impossible. That was probably what the disciples thought. But when they couldn't disprove what they had seen right before their eyes, and even savored in their mouths, their awe for Jesus grew. It was a miracle. But how did Jesus do it? Well . . . that remains a real mystery. But the real significance lay in the fact that Jesus' public ministry began at that wedding in Cana. The world would never be the same again.

For the full account of the wedding at Cana, read John 2.

CURIOUS CONNECTIONS

TALL TALES
Throughout the Old Testament we find evidence of a mysterious race of giants. Where they came from remains cloaked in uncertainty; what eventually became of these people is likewise lost in the shadows of time. In any event, they almost certainly disappeared long before the birth of Jesus.

THE NEPHILIM
Genesis 6 tells of an early race of giants that many translations say were the extraordinary beings known as the Nephilim. These mammoth beings roamed the earth before the flood, and they may have been the offspring of supernatural beings who consorted with humans (see Genesis 6:4). So large were they and their descendants that, in a later account, the Israelites said that they seemed like grasshoppers in comparison to the Nephilim. (See Numbers 13:33.)

THE REPHAIM
Another race of giants appears in the Old Testament. Known as the Rephaim, they were noted for their physical might, but they did not survive the Israelites' invasion of Canaan. Reportedly the last survivor of this race, King Og of Bashan, slept in an iron bed 13 feet long

and 6 feet wide. The Ammonites called this race the Zamzummin. (See Numbers 21:31-35.)

THE PHILISTINE GIANTS
The formidable Goliath, who stood nearly nine feet tall, was the best known of a group of giants called the descendants of Rapha. (Their relation to the Rephaim is uncertain.) A few skirmishes with these warriors appears in 2 Samuel and again in 1 Chronicles. Ishbi-benob, a descendant of the Rapha, tried to kill King David but was himself killed. David's mighty men also killed other giants, including the brother of Goliath and a warrior with six fingers on each hand and six toes on each foot! (See 2 Samuel 21:15-22; 1 Chronicles 20:4-6.)

STRANGE BUT TRUE

The Shrinking Life Spans

Why did human life expectancy decline sharply in early Bible times?

At the ripe old age of 30, most people find they cannot run the mile quite as fast as they used to. At 40, fathers begin to lose arm-wrestling matches with their kids. At 60, you may be feeling young, but a look in the mirror prevents self-deception. At 70, you have qualified for every senior-citizen discount ever invented, and people say "you're so young looking" only to coax you for a walk around the block. How did those people in the Bible live so long, when in comparison many of us grow tired and old so soon?

One of the oldest people in the Bible was Methusaleh, a man who lived 969 years, nearly a full millennium. Enoch was a mere child when his life on earth ended at age 365. Most of these people had reached our age of retirement when they merely began raising kids. How did these ancients live so long? Did they have purer air and water? Was there some type of enzyme or protein in the food they ate that gave them immunity against diseases such as cancer that plague our populations? What secret did the ancients possess that enabled them to live so long beyond our normal life span?

Although the Bible lists the names and ages of these ancient heroes, it does not provide any explanation for the longevity of their lives. We can well imagine that in those days there wasn't as much stress, the food was purer, the environment less toxic, disease less virulent, and the air less adulterated than it is today. The agricultural pace of life was most likely slower, giving the ancients time to achieve mental peace. The rat-race pace of life was still to be invented by distant descendants who looked back disbelievingly at the incredible life spans once enjoyed. Perhaps environmental and lifestyle factors explain much of the disparity between the modern person's life expectancy and the ancients of old. The fact that these extremely old people existed before the biblical account of the Flood might account for some of the differences in life expectancy. An extensive flood may have changed prehistoric atmospheric and climatic conditions that supported human existence much more readily than the environmental conditions we endure today. Still, a person's body must be unusually strong to last seven, eight, or nine centuries.

A more theological explanation is that the life expectancies declined according to a divine plan; as the earth became more populous, the need for such long life spans disappeared. Yet God's displeasure with human behavior enters into the explanation also. Genesis 6:3 contains this terse comment: "Then the Lord said, 'My Spirit will not put up with humans for such a long time, for they are only mortal flesh. In the future, they will live no more than 120 years.'" The life expectancy after Noah indeed drops sharply; Noah himself lived 950 years; his son Shem only 600; six generations later, Terah, the father of Abram, died after 148 years of life.

The reason why these ancient people lived so long continues to be a complex puzzle—and we may never have the pieces necessary to provide a complete answer.

For some ancient genealogical data, read Genesis 5.

GREAT ESCAPES

The Bible is full of stories of people who were rescued or who escaped from dangerous circumstances in the nick of time. How did they do it?

Escape	Reference
Noah and his family escaped the flood that destroyed the entire earth because they were on a giant boat.	*Genesis 6:1–8:22*
Thanks to a warning from a couple of angels, Lot's family escaped Sodom just before the entire city was destroyed.	*Genesis 19:1-29*
Isaac narrowly escaped death when an angel stopped his father from offering him as a human sacrifice.	*Genesis 22:1-19*
Joseph escaped death when his brothers decided to sell him as a slave rather than kill him.	*Genesis 37:12-36*
Joseph's family escaped a great famine when Joseph provided a home and food for them in Egypt.	*Genesis 42–47*
Moses escaped the Egyptian death sentence for all Hebrew baby boys when his mother put him in a basket and sent him down the Nile River.	*Exodus 1:1–2:10*
The Israelites escaped the pursuing Egyptian army when the Lord miraculously parted the Red Sea for his people.	*Exodus 13:17–14:31*
Balaam escaped execution at the hands of an angel because of the quick thinking of his donkey.	*Numbers 22:21-38*
David got away from King Saul's men by having his wife pretend he was sick in bed while he was really on the run.	*1 Samuel 19:11-18*
King Saul escaped death at the hands of David when David chose to merely cut off a piece of the king's robe.	*1 Samuel 24:1-22*
Four hundred Amalekite young men escaped on camels when David and his men came to destroy their land.	*1 Samuel 30:1-31*
Haman's plot to kill Mordecai backfired when the king discovered that Mordecai had prevented his assassination.	*Esther 2–7*
Shadrach, Meshach, and Abednego escaped death in a fiery furnace because the Lord protected them from the flames.	*Daniel 3:1-30*

Daniel escaped unharmed from a den of lions because God closed the lions' mouths.	*Daniel 6:1-28*
Jonah escaped from the belly of a fish when God caused the fish to vomit Jonah onto the shore.	*Jonah 1:1–2:10*
Jesus miraculously escaped from a crowd that was planning to kill him by simply walking right through the crowd.	*Luke 4:14-30*
The apostles escaped from jail when an angel of the Lord opened the doors to the cell in the middle of the night.	*Acts 5:17-29*
An angel helped the apostle Peter escape from a prison cell in which he was chained to two guards.	*Acts 12:1-19*
The apostle Paul escaped an attempt on his life when his nephew learned of the plot.	*Acts 23:12-22*

CURIOUS CONNECTIONS

FANTASTIC HEALINGS

The Bible is filled with wondrous and mysterious healings. What is fascinating about them—besides the fact that they were miraculous—is that they often were so different. How these healings happened remains a baffling mystery to doctors.

SNEEZING FROM THE DEAD

Elisha was widely known for his miracles, so it was no surprise when a distraught mother came to him after her son died. Elisha went to the dead boy's room, where he shut the door and prayed to God. He then got on the bed and stretched out over the dead boy. He placed his mouth over the boy's mouth, his eyes over the boy's eyes, and his hands over the boy's hands. The boy's body became warm, and then the boy sneezed seven times and opened his eyes. It was not, however, the actions of Elisha that brought the boy back from the dead; rather, it was his prayer to God. (See 2 Kings 4:32-37.)

SIMPLY SIMPLICITY

Some miraculous healings in the Bible amaze us because they take place so undramatically. One such healing is recorded in three of the

Gospels. We are told of a crippled man lying on a mat who was brought before Jesus as Jesus was speaking to a crowd. Jesus told the man to get up, pick up his mat, and go home. Without so much as a wave of his hand, a magic incantation, or the use of a magic wand, he restored the man to health. The paralytic picked up his mat and went home rejoicing. (See Matthew 9:6-7; Mark 2:3-12; Luke 5:18-26.)

THE CLOTHES MAKE THE MIRACLE

Jesus once performed a miracle without deliberately doing anything. The story goes as follows: A woman had been bleeding for 12 years. Doctors had been powerless to stop it. The woman came up behind Jesus and barely touched his clothes, believing it would make her well, which it did. But Jesus actually felt the power go out from him and turned to see who had touched him. He comforted the woman, who was frightened at being discovered, and declared that her faith had made her well. (See Matthew 9:18-26; Mark 5:25-34; Luke 8:43-48.)

A TOUCH OF THE HAND

Among the many miraculous healings done by Jesus in the Bible, rarely do any have a flair of showmanship or self-congratulation. The healing itself was enough, as with the case of the Jewish leader, Jairus, and his daughter. While Jairus was with Jesus and was bringing him home to cure his sick daughter, messengers announced that she had died. Jesus calmly told them to have faith and continued on to the house. When he arrived he told everyone that she was merely asleep. They laughed, but Jesus then took her by the hand and told her to get up. When she did, the laughing stopped. The girl had been raised from the dead. (See Matthew 9:18-26; Mark 5:22-43; Luke 8:41-56.)

THE SHADOW KNOWS

The leaders of the early church ministered to others through miraculous healings. The book of Acts records that the sick and crippled were brought out to the road and placed on cots and mats in hopes that the apostle known as Peter would walk by and cast his shadow on them, thus healing them. (See Acts 5:12-16.)

DID YOU KNOW?

Would God order one of his prophets to marry a prostitute?
One of the most peculiar stories in the Bible is the story of the prophet Hosea. Although an entire Bible book is named after him, not much is known about his life. The details of Hosea's marriage to the prostitute Gomer in Hosea 1 and 3 have alarmed many theologians. How could a good God command Hosea to marry a loose woman? Why would a holy God order his prophet to join himself with a thoroughly base woman? To resolve this theological conundrum, some commentators have suggested that these chapters are allegorical, merely a picture of Israel's spiritual adultery. These commentators still have to explain away the clear and straightforward language of the first chapter of Hosea: "[The Lord] said to [Hosea], 'Go and marry a prostitute'" (Hosea 1:2). Nevertheless, the imagery is poignant and unforgettable, showing Israel how God loved his people in spite of their sins.

STRANGE BUT TRUE

Bread from Heaven

What was the food that sustained the Israelites in the wilderness?

"What is it?" the famished Hebrews asked each other. No one was sure. But because everyone was asking the same question, the strange milky white ground cover was called manna. In ancient Hebrew, *manna* means "what is it?"

The desert floor east of the Red Sea was white with this mysterious substance. Like snow it lay evenly on the ground. Like frost it began to crystallize and evaporate in the midday sun. The wandering Israelites harvested the manna each day of their 40-year trek in the wilderness of Sinai.

On the day it first appeared, their leader Moses declared this unusual seedless crop "bread from heaven." Had he suffered sunstroke? Had the involuntary fast that followed their flight from Egypt been especially hard on Moses? He seemed to be talking nonsense.

"Eat dew on the dirt? You have got to be kidding!" Was it really edible? Most of the people were so hungry they spent less time questioning the dietary value of the manna than they did collecting it.

It tasted sweet like honey. It resembled coriander seed with a waferlike consistency. What is more, it satiated their desert-driven appetites. Strangely, those who tried saving additional quantities for subsequent days were disappointed. Any surplus of manna not eaten on the day it was collected began to rot by the next day. Leftover manna was an oxymoron. "You can collect only what you need to fill your stomachs each day," Moses explained.

Because the seventh day of each week was a day of rest for the Israelites, no manual labor was allowed. Therefore, no manna was to be harvested on the Sabbath. Even though manna not eaten at the end of a given day would be crawling with maggots by the next morning, on the seventh day this was not the case. Moses gave the Israelites permission to collect enough of the "Jewish dew" on the sixth day of the week to last them for two days. And sure enough, on the morning of the Sabbath the manna that had been gathered the day before was just as fresh and tasty as it had been on the sixth day. This peculiar putrefaction pattern made manna even more puzzling. Was it the atmospheric conditions of the weekdays that made the manna rot so quickly? Or did the manna gathered on Friday contain some chemical that retarded its deterioration and repelled maggots?

The manna was nutritious enough. Men and women and children survived on this bread substitute. But "bread from heaven"? Was it really a miracle food? Since these 2 million slaves had never traveled in this region before, how did they know this was not a natural phenomenon of this region of Palestine? Perhaps it was a convergence of moisture and desert plant particles that routinely coat the ground. Wild animals of the desert quite possibly had lived on the morning flakes for thousands of years. But to call it "bread from heaven"? Wasn't that a bit presumptuous? Why would God create a customized never-before-heard-of food just for a extended family of homeless nomads?

The manna God provided the Israelites in the desert kept a whole nomadic nation alive when their survival seemed in jeopardy.

It even fueled the amazing growth of the nation of Israel so that they could supplant the peoples living on the edges of the desert—the Edomites, the Midianities, and eventually the Canaanites.

You can read more about it in one of the books of Moses; begin with Exodus 16.

ONE-MAN WRECKING CREWS

Most people love to root for the underdog. Whether it's a college basketball game or the latest Hollywood action movie, the odds are stacked against the little guy. The Bible contains many stories of people who prevailed in the face of unbelievable odds. Take a look at some of these mismatched contests.

SHAMGAR VERSUS THE PHILISTINES

Judges 3 sums up the accomplishments of Shamgar in one verse. But the tale of that one verse is quite incredible. In a battle with the Philistines, Shamgar struck down hundreds of enemy soldiers with an ox goad, a long wooden rod with a metal tip used for prodding domesticated animals. Judges 3:31 records that Shamgar alone was responsible for 600 Philistine deaths!

MIGHTIEST OF THE MIGHTY

Many skilled warriors joined David before his days as king. The bravest of them became known as David's mighty men, or The Thirty, and among them were three who set themselves apart as The Three, the mightiest of the mighty. We might call Eleazar The One. On one occasion he and David challenged the Philistine army that had gathered for battle. David's forces engaged the Philistines, but the Israelites soon fell back in retreat. Eleazar, however, stood his ground. He fought the Philistines single-handedly until the entire Philistine militia had fallen to his sword, wrapped tightly in a hand so cramped he couldn't peel it off the hilt. The Israelite army returned later to plunder the bodies of the Philistine soldiers. (See 2 Samuel 23:9-10.)

JONATHAN VERSUS THE PHILISTINES

Once again the Philistines took it on the chin from a one-man vengeance squad. This time Jonathan, the son of King Saul, administered the beating. Trusting in the power of God, Jonathan, accompanied only by his armor bearer, climbed up a cliff and attacked a Philistine military outpost. After Jonathan had killed at least 20 Philistine soldiers, the rest of the Philistine army began to panic. Israelite lookouts spotted the disturbance and informed King Saul. Seizing the opportunity presented by his son's attack, Saul ordered his army to attack and soundly defeated the Philistines. (See 1 Samuel 14:1-23.)

ELIJAH VERSUS THE PROPHETS OF BAAL

Compared with Shamgar, Eleazar, and Jonathan, Elijah was a decidedly nonviolent one-man wrecking crew. The Lord used Elijah to single-handedly destroy the credibility of Baal worship. Elijah challenged 450 prophets of Baal to a contest. Elijah would prepare a sacrifice to the Lord on one altar; the prophets of Baal would prepare a sacrifice to Baal on another altar. The deity who sent fire to accept his sacrifice would be declared the God of Israel. Despite their frantic efforts (which included slashing themselves), the prophets of Baal were unable to get their god to respond. The God of Israel, on the other hand, sent a fire that consumed not only Elijah's sacrifice but the altar itself as well as the ground around it! As a result of Elijah's victory, all 450 prophets were slaughtered in the Kishon Valley. (See 1 Kings 18:16-40.)

◤ VANISHING BOOKS

At times, the Bible speaks of books or quotes from books that are not known today. Here is a list of these phantom books.

VANISHING BOOK	WHERE MENTIONED
1. The Book of the Wars of the Lord	Numbers 21:14
2. The Book of Jashar	2 Samuel 1:18
3. King David's Official Records	1 Chronicles 27:24
4. The Record of Gad the Seer	1 Chronicles 29:29
5. The Record of Nathan the Prophet	2 Chronicles 9:29
6. The Visions of Iddo the Seer	2 Chronicles 9:29

7. *The Prophecy of Ahijah from Shiloh*   2 Chronicles 9:29
8. *The Record of Jehu Son of Hanani*   2 Chronicles 20:34

BOOKS QUOTED IN THE NEW TESTAMENT
1. Traditionally entitled
   The Assumption of Moses   quoted in Jude 1:9
2. Traditionally entitled
   The Book of Enoch   quoted in Jude 1:14

AUTHORS COMMONLY ASSOCIATED WITH QUOTES IN THE NEW TESTAMENT
1. Aratus or Cleanthes   Acts 17:28
2. Menander   1 Corinthians 15:33
3. Epimendes   Titus 1:12

A LOST NEW TESTAMENT LETTER
1. Lost letter to the Corinthians   1 Corinthians 5:9

BOOKS OF THE END TIMES
1. *The Book of Life*   Psalm 69:28; Philippians 4:3
2. *The Scroll of Seven Seals*   Revelation 5:1-5
3. *The Book of Judgment*   Revelation 20:12

STRANGE BUT TRUE

Without Beginning or End

Who was the mysterious priest who ministered to Abraham?

One of the most interesting but least known characters in the Bible is the ancient priest named Melchizedek. He shows up only once during Abraham's life, but he became an archetype of the high priest that Jesus himself is most often compared to. Despite his remarkable association with Jesus, we have scant biographical data about him.

Melchizedek means "king of righteousness" or "king of Salem." Most Bible scholars believe Salem was the ancient city that became present-day Jerusalem. He is the first priest named in the Bible, and though his priesthood was not necessarily connected to Israel's priesthood descended from Aaron, Melchizedek is honored as God-fearing and even an exemplar of Jesus.

Melchizedek's name survives because, unlike many other ancient king-priests, he did not exploit his subjects—in particular, Abraham. When Abraham offered 10 percent of what he conquered to Melchizedek, the mysterious ancient priest gave Abraham a blessing and a banquet.

The author of the New Testament book of Hebrews makes much of Melchizedek, calling him "a priest forever, resembling the Son of God" (Hebrews 7:3). These are extraordinary words of praise in the Bible for a mere ancient priest. According to the author of Hebrews, he is a priest forever because he has no father or mother or any ancestors. Indeed in a book like Genesis, where the whole human race's ancestry is mapped out, there is no mention of Melchizedek's ancestors. Who was this mysterious priest-king? Who were his parents? What is his complete story? These questions have confounded biblical scholars. Was Melchizedek an angelic appearance like others described in the Bible? Or was Melchizedek merely a righteous priest who became a symbol of the righteousness the Israelites could expect from a coming Deliverer? Was Melchizedek merely a righteous leader who represented for all time a greater truth than even he imagined? Whatever the facts, we recognize that Melchizedek symbolized the covenant relationship that would come to completion in Christ.

For Melchizedek's story, read Genesis 14, Psalm 110, and Hebrews 5–7.

CURIOUS CONNECTIONS

PUZZLING PARABLES

Many of the parables found in the Gospel accounts are straightforward; the meaning and example of the Good Samaritan of Jesus' story has even made its way into a common expression in the English language. Not all of Jesus' parables, however, lend themselves to easy interpretation. These stories remind hearers that God's ways cannot always be easily discerned.

THE WORKERS IN THE VINEYARD

Jesus' listeners, most of whom came from the laboring classes, would have understood the background of this parable. A landowner, eager to harvest his crop, went out to hire workers at several points during the day. Much to the surprise of those who were hired at sunrise, all of the workers got the same wage—even those who had worked only an hour in the cool of the twilight. It seemed unfair to Jesus' audience as well. Is this how God rewards people? Those who jumped to a hasty conclusion likely missed the point: The parable really teaches us about God's generosity, even to those who find him at the last hour. It masterfully points out that God is just (he pays all workers fairly) as well as merciful. (See Matthew 20:1-16.)

THE SHREWD MANAGER

One parable that Jesus told only to his disciples concerned a rich man and his business manager. The underling had been wasteful and was in danger of losing his job. After receiving a warning and being called to give an account of himself, the manager cut some shady deals with the rich man's debtors, hoping for their favor when he found himself out of a job. Strangely, Jesus did not tell the parable to condemn unethical behavior. Quite the contrary. The owner commended the servant, and Jesus told his disciples, "I tell you, use your worldly resources to benefit others and make friends. In this way, your generosity stores up a reward for you in heaven." Although the point of the parable is still debated, one may infer that one may use worldly wealth wisely to do good. By lowering the debt others owed, the servant and the master gain a more favorable standing with those creditors. (See Luke 16:1-12.)

THE PERSISTENT WIDOW

Jesus had many intriguing things to say about prayer, but one parable that he told his disciples had an interesting twist. A widow tormented a judge time after time, asking for justice against her adversaries. Time after time she went away frustrated. Finally, he grew so sick of the annoyance that—not from his sense of godliness or righteousness but simply to be rid of her—he granted her request. "I'm going to see that she gets justice, because she is wearing me out with her constant requests!" Jesus makes an immediate correlation to God's answering his people's prayers. So was he suggesting that God considered repeated petitions as annoyances to be answered so he could get some peace of mind? Actually, the point of this parable is the necessity of faithfulness in prayer. If repeated requests could wear down a heartless judge, how much more would a loving God respond to our fervent pleas? (See Luke 18:1-8.)

STRANGE BUT TRUE

The Queen's Visit

Who was the royal visitor so taken with Solomon's power and wisdom?

Early in his reign, Solomon, the successor to King David, enjoyed one of the greatest reputations of any person in history: he was wise *and* charming! So evident was Solomon's wisdom that foreign delegations would travel to investigate the news they had heard on the trade routes and through international gossip columnists. One of those visitors was the mysterious queen of Sheba.

Of her real identity science and archaeology know very little. She may have come from Yemen, where rule by royal queenships was common. She may have been a sage herself, eager to test her wisdom against Israel's king. To conclude that she was impressed understates the point. The queen was overwhelmed indeed, and Solomon likewise seems to have been delightfully shaken by the queen's aura.

Ethiopian tradition picks up where archaeology leaves off. According to traditional history, this amazing woman known as Queen Makeda returned from her tour of Jerusalem with gifts in kind plus a pregnancy, which would not be so out of line with Solomon's reputation with foreign women (1 Kings 11:1). The first great king of that part of the world was Menelik I, Solomon's son, born as a result of the queen's state visit. Tradition also reports that Menelik returned to Jerusalem at age 22 to learn the Scriptures and to carry the faith back to his own emerging kingdom.

Royal tradition is both hard to prove and often hard to believe.

But we do know that a woman of wealth, power, and curiosity once made a long journey to verify for herself the reputation of another young ruler and came away convinced that his dash and daring were more than equal to the rumors she had heard. We just don't know—exactly—who she was!

For more on the Queen of Sheba, read 1 Kings 10.

CURIOUS CONNECTIONS

THE RISE AND FALL OF THE TEMPLE

The long and dramatic history of the Temple in Jerusalem continues to intrigue scholars and laypeople alike. In Israel's history, three temples have been built, each of them eventually destroyed. Only a portion of the western wall—the famous Wailing Wall where orthodox Jews gather to pray—remains today.

SOLOMON'S TEMPLE

Solomon, the third king of Israel, earned renown as the wisest and wealthiest man of his day. To him came the honor of building the first Temple for the Israelite people. (David, who purchased the site for the Temple, was not allowed to build it because he had shed much blood—see 1 Chronicles 28:3.) The magnificent structure took 13 years to build. It was adorned with precious stones throughout. Gold covered the ceiling beams, doors, door frames, and walls. Solomon dedicated the Temple in a magnificent ceremony, which culminated when the Ark was brought into the Holy of Holies and the glory of the Lord filled the Temple. The Temple survived several raids but was completely destroyed by the Babylonians in 586 B.C. (See 1 Kings 6–10; 2 Chronicles 3–5.)

THE SECOND TEMPLE

Standing for nearly 500 years, the Second Temple survived longer than either Solomon's or Herod's Temple. Built by the Jewish exiles after their return to Jerusalem from captivity in Babylon, this house of worship was not as grand as the house of worship that Solomon had built. Many of the expensive furnishings could not be replaced, and the sacred chest, the Ark of the Covenant, had disappeared. This Temple's completion was nonetheless a moving moment for the exiles, who wept for joy—and for the loss of what had been the glory of the first Temple. The Roman general Pompey besieged and destroyed the Second Temple in 63 B.C. (See Ezra 1; 5:2-3, 8-10.)

HEROD'S TEMPLE

Herod, ruler of Judea, was a foreigner and despised by the Jewish people. In an attempt to win their goodwill, he began rebuilding the Temple in Jerusalem about 19 B.C. The main structure took about ten years to complete, but it would not be entirely finished until A.D. 64. Just six years later, the Roman army leveled Herod's Temple to complete its suppression of a Jewish revolt. (See Matthew 24:1-2.)

EZEKIEL'S TEMPLE

The Jewish prophet Ezekiel, who wrote in exile in Babylon, had a vision in which he saw a glorious temple. Some insist he was merely recalling the majesty of Solomon's Temple. But his description is at odds with what we know about Solomon's Temple, so others have suggested that Ezekiel was in effect proposing plans for a new temple to be built by the returning exiles. Others believe that his temple is an allegorical description that predicts the blessings God would give his people. Another interpretation posits that Ezekiel's prophecy describes Jesus' return and the setting up of his messianic kingdom. But the questions remain, and the meaning of Ezekiel's temple remains a mystery. (See Ezekiel 40–43.)

MIGHTY WARRIORS

Ancient warriors of the Bible. They defeated thousands—even tens of thousands. How did they do it? What was the source of their strength? In most cases, their skills were complemented by divine strength and guidance. The source of their victories was God himself.

Person	Experience	Reference
Abishai	A member of David's cadre of 30 warriors—a group of elite fighting men	*1 Samuel 26:6-9*
Abner	King Saul's army commander who later became a victim of a vengeful Joab	*1 Samuel 14:50; 17:55*
Abram	Led 318 trained men to battle against four kings who plundered Sodom and Gomorrah, where Lot had settled. He recovered their goods and his nephew.	*Genesis 14:11-17*
Barak	Defeated the Canaanites, led by Sisera. His reluctance to go to battle without the prophetess Deborah resulted in his being denied the ultimate victory—the death of Sisera. The honor went to a woman instead.	*Judges 4*
David	A skilled shepherd and fearless warrior who became king. Defeated the giant Goliath, the champion of the Philistines, with a sling and five rocks. Described as "a man of blood."	*1 Samuel 16:18; 17; 2 Samuel 8; 10; 1 Chronicles 28:3*
Gideon	Sent to fight against the Midianites, although he was reluctant to do so at first. Went to battle with a ragtag group of 300 men against thousands of Midianites—and won.	*Judges 6–8*
Goliath	Champion of the Philistines. A man over 9 feet tall. His armor alone weighed over 125 pounds. Taunted the Israelites and their God, which led to his death.	*1 Samuel 17*
Jephthah	This Gileadite went to war against Israel's enemies, the Ammonites, and defeated them (he devastated 20 towns); became a judge or leader of Israel.	*Judges 11:1-33*

Jonathan	Son of Saul; with his armor bearer attacked a Philistine outpost single-handedly; later died in battle.	*1 Samuel 14:1-14; 31:2-3; 2 Samuel 1:22-25*
Joshua	Selected to lead the Israelites into the Promised Land after Moses. Led the Israelites in several battles with various Canaanite groups to gain control of the land. Defeated the armies of 31 kings.	*Joshua 1–11*
Nimrod	A mighty warrior/hunter, considered the standard by which great hunters were measured. He built cities like Nineveh, Rehoboth Ir, Calah in Assyria. He was a descendant of Ham, son of Noah.	*Genesis 10:8-9*
Saul	Picked as Israel's first king; chosen to deliver Israel from the Philistines; was killed in battle.	*1 Samuel 9:16-17; 11:8-11; 31:2-3*
Pekah	This son of Remaliah once killed 120,000 soldiers in Judah when Judah turned away from God.	*2 Chronicles 28:6*
Samson	A judge of Israel known for having incredible physical strength; once killed 1,000 Philistines with the jawbone of a donkey; killed a lion with his bare hands; knocked down the pillars of a Philistine temple, killing 3,000 men and women as well as himself	*Judges 14:5-6; 15:15-17; 16:23-30*
Sisera	Canaanite general; had 900 iron chariots; was greatly feared until his defeat by Barak and the Israelite army.	*Judges 4:2-3*
Uriah	A Hittite warrior in David's army; David exposed him to certain death so that he could take his wife.	*2 Samuel 11*
Zadok	Described as "a brave young warrior."	*1 Chronicles 12:28*
Zicri	An Ephraimite warrior, killed Maaseiah, the king's son; Azrikam, the officer in charge of the palace; and Elkanah, second to the king.	*2 Chronicles 28:7*

Dungeons and Disciples

A prisoner disappears but leaves no evidence

A jailbreak! Early one April day, Herod's royal guards were left in a panic. One of the most important prisoners left in their charge, Peter, had disappeared without a trace.

The facts were simple. The officer in charge had gone over and over them. He had left a total of 16 soldiers, four squads of four soldiers, to guard Peter in the depths of the Fortress of Antonia. Four soldiers were to guard Peter at all times—one chained to his left wrist, and one chained to his right. The other two were to stand watch outside. To make sure no one fell asleep, these guards were to rotate four times that night with another set of well-rested guards. Nothing could go wrong—or so the officer in charge thought.

But the next day, Peter was gone! The last shift of guards was still there; the chains remained. The ground still showed the outline of where Peter had sat. But where Peter had gone or how he had freed himself from those heavy chains remained a puzzle. There was no sign of a forced exit: a broken latch or a hastily dug tunnel. Nothing! The guards officially denied seeing or hearing anything. But unofficially, some of them spoke of a mysterious bright light, which had put them in a strange trance. How could Peter have escaped? Not even a seasoned escape artist could pull this off.

A careful investigation, headed by Herod himself, led nowhere. Herod could only conclude that it was an inside job. One of the guards had to have helped Peter escape. Such treachery deserved severe punishment, and all 16 guards were led away to their swift execution.

Years later, Peter reemerged in Jerusalem. His version of what happened that night was extraordinary, explaining in part why Herod's investigation was so futile.

According to Peter, it was late at night, and he was fast asleep, when suddenly a bright light lit up his damp prison cell. A bright figure, which resembled a man, ordered him to get up and get dressed. The man appeared so extraordinary—his face glowed and his long white robe shone—that Peter thought he was still asleep, seeing a vision (something that had happened to him before; see Acts 10). But when he got up, he could feel the cold steel chains unlatch themselves, freeing his sore wrists. The angelic creature led Peter through the dark corridors of Antonia and past two guards on watch, who strangely did not seem to notice that they were even there. And before Peter knew what was happening, he was walking through the heavy iron gates of the fortress, which seemed to open at the angel's touch. Peter was out on the main street leading to the middle of Jerusalem. He took a deep breath of cool, night air and turned to his companion. But the man was gone . . . and the adjacent streets were abandoned. Peter decided to return to his companions in the faith, who were praying for him in a nearby home. So astonished was the girl who answered the door that she forget to let Peter in! The whole church rejoiced in the deliverance of the supposedly doomed disciple.

For more information, see Acts 12.

C U R I O U S   C O N N E C T I O N S

WINNING AGAINST ALL ODDS
The Bible tells many stories of people achieving astounding victories against incredible odds. How these people escaped from certain death or defeat is a baffling puzzle that even the most dedicated inquirer cannot solve.

THE ARMY THAT COULDN'T SEE STRAIGHT
The Arameans were at war with Israel. They tried frequently to set up ambushes, but the prophet Elisha would tell the king of Israel about it, and the soldiers would have time to escape. So the king of Aram got angry with Elisha and decided to go after him. When he found out where Elisha was, he sent his troops to surround the city at night. The next morning the Aramean forces attacked, and as they did, Elisha prayed and asked God to strike the men blind. Instantly the Aramean soldiers all became sightless. Elisha went out and told them that they were on the wrong road and had attacked the wrong city. He then led them to Samaria, Israel's capital. As soon as they entered the city gates, he prayed for their sight to be restored. They were captured. The king

of Israel then gave them a feast and sent them home, and the Arameans stopped their attacks on Israel. (See 2 Kings 6:8-23.)

HANDS UP!

A short time after the miracle at the Red Sea, the Israelites encountered resistance again—this time from the Amalekites, a fierce people that inhabited the desert land of Sinai. Moses summoned Joshua to assemble the Israelites for war. The ensuing battle turned into a seesaw event. As long as Moses held up his staff with his hands, the Israelites prevailed. But when he lowered his hands, the Amalekites would push back the Israelites. Finally, Aaron and Hur had Moses sit on a rock while they held up his hands. By sunset, Israel had crushed the invading tribes. A grateful Moses built an altar to the Lord at that site. (See Exodus 17:10-16.)

DAYLIGHT SAVINGS

The resounding victory that Joshua gained over the Amorites resulted from a series of remarkable supernatural interventions. Joshua had traveled to the besieged city of Gibeon to rescue its inhabitants. Scripture declares that the Amorite armies were surprised by Joshua's rapid arrival, and they panicked. Their ranks broke and soldiers fled on foot, where they were pounded by a hailstorm that took more lives than had fallen in battle that day. More astounding was the answer of Joshua's prayer. Before the battle, he had earnestly asked God to make the sun stand still over Gibeon. And Scripture tells us that the sun indeed stopped its motion until the Amorites were defeated. The concluding statement of this passage sums up the amazing event: "Never before or since has there been a day like that one, when the Lord answered such a request from a human being." (See Joshua 10:9-14.)

WATER WATER ANYWHERE

Humans cannot live without water. In the arid regions of the Middle East, traveling without water invited great risk, even death. So what were God's people to do when water was nowhere in sight? Here are miraculous stories of water that came from the most unexpected places.

DYING OF THIRST: PART 1

Early during their march in the wilderness, the Israelites began complaining to their leader, Moses, about the lack of water in the desert. They had just escaped from Egypt, but the Israelites apparently had short-term memories: they forgot about God's goodness to them and whined as if God was no longer interested in their welfare. Exodus records that Moses asked God what to do, and God had him take the elders to a rock at Mount Sinai and strike it with his staff. From the rock came water for the people to drink. Even so, the place became known as Massah—"the place of testing"—because of the Israelites' lack of faith. (See Exodus 17:1-7.)

DYING OF THIRST: PART 2

Several years after the incident at Massah, the Israelites again tested God's patience. Arriving at Kadesh in the wilderness of Zin, they complained because of the lack of water. They challenged Moses, their leader, and declared that they would be better off dead. God told Moses to simply speak to a rock nearby in the presence of the people, and water would gush out for them and their livestock. Moses, perhaps angry because of yet another challenge to his leadership, instead struck the rock with his staff. The water burst forth, and the people drank their fill. But because he had acted contrary to God's instruction, Moses was not allowed to enter the Promised Land. (See Numbers 20:1-13.)

A SPRING FOR SAMSON

He sat on the ground, exhausted. Samson, the great hero of the Israelites, had struck down 1,000 Philistines using only the jawbone of a donkey. But the ordeal had drained him. Crying out, Samson complained to God that he was dying of thirst. Suddenly a spring of water gushed from a hollow in the ground, and Samson drank until he was satisfied. In gratitude, Samson named the place Lehi, "The Spring of the One Who Cried Out." (See Judges 15:18-19.)

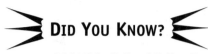

DID YOU KNOW?

Did Michal die childless?
The tragic life of Michal, King Saul's daughter, was filled with turmoil and disappointment. First, she fell in love with the young and courageous David. To obtain her hand in marriage, David didn't shrink from killing 100 Philistines. But Saul's murderous rage kept the two lovers apart, forcing David to flee—without his new wife, Michal. Michal was later betrothed to another man. But when David ascended to the throne of Israel, he claimed her as his lawful wife.

Michal, however, experienced discontent in her marriage to David. She protested David's dancing before the Ark of God. We infer that because of her angry outburst, Michal was afflicted with barrenness. Although 2 Samuel 6:23 emphatically states that Michal died childless, some ancient Hebrew manuscripts assert that Michal's five sons were among those killed by the Gibeonites (2 Samuel 21:8). Most manuscript experts consider the mention of Michal in this passage as a copyist's error. The woman who lost her sons was likely Michal's sister, Merab.

 FAQs (frequently asked questions)

MIRACLES

Doesn't the idea of miracles conflict with the natural laws that govern this world?
In recent centuries, science has made great strides in understanding how our world works. From Newton's discovering the law of gravity to Einstein's discovering the theory of relativity, science has explained and defined the laws that govern the universe. Coupled with the astonishing progress of science, however,

has been a growing skepticism of the supernatural and of supernatural events such as miracles.

Some of this skepticism is misguided. The existence of natural laws does not preclude the reality of miracles, and vice versa. There are several different ways to understand what miracles are, but none of these explanations discounts the existence of natural laws. A miracle is, by definition, an event that is not natural or ordinary. These events are direct acts of God that either counter ordinary natural forces or break the natural laws in place. Some have suggested that miracles might even be a manifestation of unknown natural laws, which God uses to show his power.

In any case, a miracle is an exceptional event that originates in God's will and points to God (Psalm 77:14; Hebrews 2:4). Since a miracle is not a part of our ordinary experience, it has not been subject to the same type of scrutiny natural phenomena have endured. This is why science doesn't have an explanation for miracles—and probably never will.

Why did Jesus perform miracles?
The Bible records a number of miracles performed by Jesus— from turning water into wine to healing the lepers and the blind (John 2:1-11; 9:1-41). Through these miracles, Jesus changed people's lives forever. A blind person could see. A leper was healed and reunited with mainstream society. The results pointed to the type of God Jesus was revealing—a compassionate God who loved to liberate people and reconcile them.

A miracle's primary purpose, however, was to function as a sign of the divine origin of Jesus' message. Jesus performed many miracles among the people in order to prove to the people that he was from God—in fact, that he is the Son of God. (See John 2:11; 6:14; Acts 2:22-33.)

Some Gospel passages say that Jesus sometimes chose not to perform miracles because the people didn't have faith. What is the connection?
In his hometown of Nazareth, Jesus didn't perform miracles because the people there lacked faith (Matthew 13:53-58). Later,

Jesus enabled Peter to walk on the water. But the text states that Peter's doubts caused him to sink. When Jesus helped him out of the water, he rebuked Peter for being of little faith (Matthew 14:31). Why was Jesus' ability to perform miracles hindered by a lack of faith or trust in God?

The explanation lies in the purpose of miracles. They are signs from God to authenticate either a person as God's special servant or the message being preached (Hebrews 2:1-4). If the one benefiting from the miracle does not acknowledge God as the originator of this great event or seek out God's assistance, then a supernatural event is pointless. If a person is unwilling to recognize a miracle as a sign of God's presence, God's extraordinary activity will go completely unnoticed. This is why Jesus made it clear that his miracles were tied to a person's faith in God. (See Matthew 9:2, 22-29; 15:28; Mark 5:34; Luke 17:5-6, 19; 18:42.)

*H*EAVENLY
HOSTS

Angels and Other
Supernatural Wonders

Strange Lights and Mysterious Voices

What happened to Saul on the road to Damascus remains a mystery

When he set out that morning, Saul was on a grim mission. He was on his way to Damascus to capture as many Christians as he could round up and bring them back to Jerusalem in chains.

The Christians were getting stronger and more numerous every day, with their claims that a teacher named Jesus was the promised Messiah. To Saul, an orthodox Jew trained by the great religious teacher Gamaliel, that was heresy. To stop this upstart movement once and for all, Saul had determined to become a one-man police force, gathering up heretical Christians wherever he could find them—from the marketplace to their very own homes. Saul hated all Christians and everything they stood for. He vowed to stop them all if he could. According to Saul's thinking, there was no place in all of Israel that should tolerate this heretical sect.

But Saul never completed his mission. As he neared Damascus, a brilliant light suddenly blinded him, knocking him to his knees. A booming voice spoke out of the air. And then, as he picked himself up off the ground, he couldn't see! Completely blind, he had to be led by the hand to Damascus, where he spent three days without food and water. Later, after a visit with Ananias, he just as suddenly regained his sight.

After that fateful day, Saul was never the same. Saul, who now called himself Paul, became a great preacher and teacher and led several long, dangerous journeys that spread Christianity throughout the Roman Empire. Paul wrote several books of the New Testament, many of them from a prison cell, where he had been sentenced for preaching about Jesus.

What really happened on the Damascus road? The eyewitnesses were just as mystified as those who heard about it later. They saw the blinding light and heard the voice, but saw no one and were at a loss to explain it. They were dumbfounded.

What was the bright light that stopped Paul in his tracks and knocked him to the ground? Where did it come from? Whose mysterious voice spoke to him, and what did it say?

Many thought the sun reflecting off a shiny object created a beam of light that struck Paul in the eyes and caused temporary blindness. Some said the voice was only the murmuring of the wind through the hills and valleys along the road. Others said Paul must have suffered heatstroke, which caused him to have hallucinations.

Paul's own explanation was just as strange and fascinating. He said that when the light knocked him to the ground he heard a voice saying, "Saul, Saul, why are you persecuting me?" When Paul asked who was speaking, the voice answered, "I am Jesus, the one you are persecuting. Now get up and go into the city and await my instructions."

This encounter radically changed Paul's life forever. Once determined to wipe Christianity off the face of the earth, he now became a man whose sole passion in life was to tell every person in the world about Jesus.

For more information, see Acts 9; 22.

CURIOUS CONNECTIONS

ARMED ANGELS

From colorful coffee-table books to cards, angels are pictured as radiant, gracious creatures. People usually associate angels with compassion. Angels are rarely pictured as rigid and stern, armed with long, sharp swords. Yet in a number of passages, the Bible does picture angels as armed and dangerous. In fact, most angelic encounters in the Bible leave people cowering in absolute fear.

THE ANGELIC GUARDIANS OF EDEN

The first mention of angelic beings in the Bible occurs after Adam and Eve had sinned against God. Because of their sin, God exiled Adam and Eve from Paradise. To make sure no person would ever enter the Garden again, the Lord dispatched angelic beings called cherubim to guard the place. Cherubim are angelic beings who look like people but have four wings (see Ezekiel 1:5-10; 10:1-22). According to the Bible, these fearsome angels guarded the Garden. To assist them in this task, God gave them each a flaming sword, which flashed back and forth across the entrance to Paradise. No person could enter the Garden without facing certain death. (See Genesis 3:24.)

THE ANGELIC COMMANDER OF GOD'S ARMY

Sword-bearing angels may inspire awe, but the fear is diminished if they are fighting on your side! Joshua, the great military commander of the Israelites, experienced this. He had to conquer the great walled city of Jericho. But its ancient defenses were formidable. One day when Joshua was surveying Jericho, he looked up and saw an angel with his sword drawn. Joshua reacted as a military man would. "Are you a friend or foe?" he queried. "Neither," the man answered. The angel explained that he was the commander of God's heavenly armies. Joshua immediately fell to the ground in deep reverence. Like Moses had done, he removed his sandals, for he stood on holy ground (Joshua 5:13-15). After this encounter, Joshua would lead his army to victory over Jericho.

THE ANGEL OF DEATH

The angel of death (though not specifically called such) is mentioned a number of times in the Bible. All the firstborn sons in Egypt suffered his fatal stroke during the first Passover (Exodus 12:11-13, 28-30). Balaam narrowly averted the angel's deadly sword (Numbers 22:31-34). But 70,000 Israelites were cut down by this angel during King David's reign. David had sinned by counting his fighting men and taking pride in his military might. With one lethal campaign by the angel of death, God showed how helpless David truly was (2 Samuel 24:10-25). The only defense David had against this mighty, sword-bearing angel was prayer to God. David begged God for mercy, and God gave it. He stopped the armed angel on the threshing floor of Araunah. This spot became the site of Solomon's Temple, and as such, a symbol of God's mercy.

◣◣◣ THE ANGEL OF THE LORD

A mysterious messenger from God—the angel of the Lord—appears often in the Old Testament. Much debate has revolved around the exact identity of this mysterious messenger. Was this angel God himself or perhaps a preincarnate form of Christ? Whoever he might be, it is clear this being commanded considerable respect from humans.

1. An angel of the Lord told Hagar that she was pregnant with Abraham's son (Genesis 16:1-16).
2. An angel of the Lord stopped Abraham just as he was about to sacrifice his son Isaac (Genesis 22:1-19).
3. An angel of the Lord appeared to Moses in a burning bush and instructed him to lead the Israelites out of Egypt (Exodus 3:1-22).
4. An angel of the Lord stood poised to kill Balaam, whose life was spared because of the actions of his donkey (Numbers 22:21-38).
5. An angel of the Lord went to Bokim and told the Israelites he wouldn't drive the pagan people out of the land of Canaan because they had made treaties with the people (Judges 2:1-7).
6. An angel of the Lord instructed Gideon to lead an Israelite attack against the mighty Midianites (Judges 6:11-40).
7. An angel of the Lord revealed to Manoah and his wife that they would have a son named Samson (Judges 13:1-25).
8. An angel of the Lord strengthened and encouraged Elijah (1 Kings 19:1-9).

9. An angel of the Lord killed 185,000 Assyrian soldiers in one night (2 Kings 19:35-36).

10. An angel of the Lord interpreted a series of visions for the prophet Zechariah (Zechariah 1:7-6:15).

STRANGE BUT TRUE

The Flying Prophet

How did Elijah enter heaven?

Long before anyone imagined planes leaving the ground, a man was reported flying in heaven. Was this alien abduction? Did Elijah know the physics of air travel thousands of years ago?

Here are the facts: When Elijah, one of the most famous of Israel's prophets, was nearing the end of his life, he walked toward Bethel with Elisha.

On a warm day sometime around 848 B.C., the prophet Elijah tested his understudy by suggesting that the younger prophet stay behind. But Elisha insisted on staying with Elijah. He knew something extraordinary was going to happen. But he did not know what.

Then Elijah turned to go. He struck the Jordan River with his cloak, separating the waters. They crossed together. They shared a few words. Elijah asked what he could do for Elisha. Elisha, perhaps a bit nervous, waited for the sign of what was coming.

What came was a chariot of fire descending from the sky. In a whirlwind the chariot drawn by horses of fire swooped Elijah up, up, and away. With his cloak over his mouth and his hands shading his eyes, Elisha strained to keep his teacher in sight. But in seconds the scene was calm again—high clouds, blue sky, and hot, summer sunshine, just like any other day.

What happened to Elijah? How could he have ascended into the heavens without the aid of modern aircraft?

We know that air has weight and that the force called gravity causes objects heavier than air to stick close to earth. We also know that with proper fuel and propulsion, heavier-than-air objects like a jumbo aircraft can defy gravity as long as the fuel keeps burning and the jet fans keep spinning. Did Elijah know something about aerodynamics that other people of his day could only dream about?

We can only guess at the physics explaining Elijah's unusual flight. The chariotlike object was obviously not bound by gravity's laws. Propelled by some force unknown at the time, it took Elijah into outer space. That is remarkable engineering. Not only did this open chariot travel at lightning speed, it traveled in a certain direction guided by some unseen intelligent force.

Elisha named that unseen force—the God of Israel. God himself had gathered up the righteous prophet Elijah to his heavenly home. Elisha's response was praise to God. He went home, but he was a different man—a man empowered by this unseen force to accomplish extraordinary acts such as bringing a poor widow's son back to life.

For more on Elijah's spaceflight, read 2 Kings 2.

CuRiOuS CoNNEcTiOnS

PEOPLE RAISED FROM THE DEAD

Death remains an enduring mystery. Our technology can tell us nothing about what awaits the person who dies. Yet tales of near-death experiences abound. The Bible has a number of intriguing stories about people not only surviving a near-death experience but actually coming back from the dead. These are people whose stories continue to amaze us.

THE MAN WHO TOUCHED ELISHA'S BONES

In the years that followed the death of Elisha the prophet, the people of Israel were plagued by Moabite raiders who invaded their land every spring. One such raid occurred during an Israelite burial ceremony. Fearing the marauding Moabites, members of the burial party hurriedly threw the corpse into the tomb of Elisha. The Bible reports that as soon as the corpse touched the bones of Elisha, the dead man revived. (See 2 Kings 13:20-21.)

LAZARUS

Mary and Martha were two of Jesus' most faithful followers. When their brother, Lazarus, became ill, the two women sent immediately for Jesus. Yet when Jesus heard the news of Lazarus's illness, he chose to stay where he was for two days before going to visit the sick man. By the time Jesus got to Bethany, Lazarus was dead. In fact, he had been buried for four days. Jesus ordered that the stone be removed from in front of Lazarus's tomb. When the stone was rolled away, Jesus prayed and then called in a loud voice, "Lazarus, come out!" To the astonishment of the crowd, Lazarus did just that—still wrapped in his graveclothes. (See John 11:1-44.)

EUTYCHUS

On the last day of the apostle Paul's visit to Troas, he and some Christians of the city talked late into the night in an upstairs meeting room. A young man named Eutychus was present at the meeting. Apparently Eutychus was sitting on a window ledge listening to the apostle. As the hour grew later, Eutychus began to nod off. Somehow he lost his balance and fell to his death three stories below. Paul rushed downstairs, threw himself on the young man's corpse, and then announced, "He's alive!" And so he was. After a late meal, the people of the city took the presumably now wide-awake young man home. (See Acts 20:7-12.)

DID YOU KNOW?

What do angels eat?

Angels are usually pictured as flying, blowing trumpets, and speaking to startled men and women. Artists rarely depict angels eating, although the Bible plainly mentions the feasts and sacrifices that were presented to heavenly visitors. Lot set a great feast—complete with fresh bread—before the two angels that visited him (Genesis 19:1-3). Abraham offered a roasted calf, cheese curds, and milk to the three angelic men who visited him (Genesis 18:6-8). Manoah, Samson's father, offered a roasted goat to an angel. But the angel refused to eat it, telling Manoah to sacrifice the goat as a praise offering to God instead (Judges

13:12-21). Although it is not clear whether angels eat in heaven, the Bible does hint at heavenly food. Psalmists describe manna— the white, crisp wafers the Israelites ate in the wilderness—as the food of angels (Psalm 78:24-25). Jesus speaks of eating and drinking with his disciples in heaven (Luke 22:15, 30).

STRANGE BUT TRUE

Road to Recognition

Two travelers can't see the truth

They say that misery loves company. On a country road long ago, one miserable pair got some very unexpected company.

Within a week after the death of Jesus, two of his followers were walking on the road to the village called Emmaus, just outside Jerusalem. Lost in grief and expressing to each other how much they missed Jesus, they were startled when a stranger joined them. He asked them what they were talking about.

"What? Are you the only person in Jerusalem who hasn't heard what's been going on?" replied the one named Cleopas. When the stranger professed ignorance of current events, they described their teacher, Jesus. They told how they'd hoped he was the Savior that Jews had been awaiting for centuries, but that he had been arrested and violently killed on a cross—first-century capital punishment at its worst.

Cleopas and his companion were confused as well as sad. There had been talk of Jesus' rising from the dead, evidently rumors started by some women. Some of Jesus' followers had checked out the tomb, but they had found nothing. Not even a body!

The stranger was actually the very man they were mourning, but somehow they couldn't see him for what he was. As they walked on toward Emmaus, he proceeded to explain the prophecies concerning his identity and work on earth. Still they didn't recognize him. They reached Cleopas's home and invited the stranger to stay for dinner.

Finally, as Jesus broke bread with them, recognition dawned. They realized that these same hands had broken bread with his followers for the Passover meal the night before he had died. But just as their eyes were opened, he vanished.

Why didn't these two distraught travelers recognize Jesus from the start? Was their grief so great that they could hardly look into his face? Or was his appearance mysteriously changed, veiled to their eyes? What form did Jesus take? Was he merely an apparition?

Jesus' appearance to the two disciples marked the first of many appearances of Jesus to his followers in the days following his crucifixion. Evidently liberated from a human body, Jesus could appear and disappear. Yet unlike a mere spirit, Jesus could eat and drink. He was alive. No one knows the exact nature of Jesus' resurrected body. But hundreds of disciples, including this pair who were walking on the Emmaus road, attested that Jesus was alive. They had seen him, touched him, and even heard him. It was the message that Jesus was alive that motivated the early disciples to travel around the world telling others about Jesus. Only something as extraordinary as a man raised from the dead can adequately explain the commitment of those early disciples to Jesus and his message of Good News to the world.

For the full account of what happened on the Emmaus road, read Luke 24:13-35.

CURIOUS CONNECTIONS

FABULOUS FOOD
Eating food is a common, everyday activity. But in times of famine or in desolate deserts, obtaining food can be a gargantuan task. The Bible describes a number of occasions in which obtaining food to eat was truly a stupendous feat. Sometimes the food came from a mysterious, heavenly source. Sometimes ordinary food lasted an extraordinarily long time. Yet, in all of these cases, the people marveled over the food that kept them alive.

A MEAL THAT KEPT ON GOING ... AND GOING ... AND GOING
During the bleak days of a severe famine, the prophet Elijah went to a widow to ask for some food and water. The widow told him that all

she had was a handful of flour and a little cooking oil. It was just enough for one last meal. Afterwards she and her son were going to sit down and wait to die. But Elijah promised that she would live through the famine if she used her flour and oil to bake him a loaf of bread. Each day after that, the woman was amazed to find enough flour and oil to feed herself, her son, and Elijah. No matter how much she used, there was always a little left in the containers for another day. (See 1 Kings 17:1-16.)

ANGEL FOOD?

Elijah was tired, hungry, and thirsty. He was fleeing for his life from the evil Queen Jezebel. But in the middle of the desert, he collapsed in utter exhaustion. He didn't have an ounce of energy left. Under a scrawny bush, he fell fast asleep. Suddenly, an angel touched him, awakening him from his deep sleep. "Get up and eat," the angel said. When Elijah opened his eyes, he saw bread baking on hot stones and a jar of water. He ate and drank until he was full and then went back to sleep. Again the angel shook him awake. "Get up and eat some more, for there is a long journey ahead of you," he told Elijah. Elijah obeyed. Once again he ate all the food that was before him. (See 1 Kings 19:1-9.)

DEATH IN THE POT

Elisha was entertaining a group of prophets when he ordered his servant to start making a stew for his guests. The servant obeyed, gathering all kinds of wild herbs, squash, and vines from the fields nearby. He diced these and threw them into a pot of boiling water. After he had finished the stew, he served it to the prophets. But as the prophets began to taste it, they cried out, "Man of God, there's poison in this stew!" meaning that poisonous plants had mistakenly been added to the ingredients. Elisha remained calm. He sprinkled some flour into the pot and ordered his servants to serve the stew to his guests again. The hungry guests ate the stew, but mysteriously no one died or was even sickened by the deadly ingredients. (See 2 Kings 4:38-41.)

MYSTERIOUS MESSENGERS

According to Hebrews 13:2, "some [people] . . . have entertained angels without realizing it!" (TLB). This is certainly true of many people in the Bible. Throughout history, God used these "mysterious messengers" to bring messages of hope, life, and death to his people.

Person Visited	Reason	Reference
Abraham	Three men, two of whom were angels and one possibly God himself, appeared to assure Abraham that he and his wife would have a child in their old age. An angel later appeared to him on Mount Moriah to prevent him from sacrificing his son.	*Genesis 18; 22:11-18*
Apostles	They were arrested for preaching, but an angel released them from prison.	*Acts 5:18-19*
Balaam	Summoned by Balak, king of Moab, to curse the Israelites. On his way to visit the king, an angel blocked his path, but he didn't recognize it until his donkey spoke to him.	*Numbers 22:21-35*
Cornelius	Cornelius, a righteous Gentile, saw a vision and heard an angel speak.	*Acts 10:3-7*
Daniel	Claimed an angel shut the mouths of the lions when he was thrown in the den of lions. Later, he had a number of visits from a messenger called Gabriel, who had been sent by God to interpret Daniel's visions of end times.	*Daniel 6:22; 8:15-27; 9:19-27; 10:1–12:13*
David	His disobedience led God to send an angel to bring a plague to the people. Some 70,000 people died.	*2 Samuel 24:15-17; 1 Chronicles 21:12-27*
Elijah	A depressed Elijah was twice visited	*1 Kings 19:5-7*

by an angel who brought him food
and drink.

Gideon	An angel of the Lord was sent to Gideon to call him to battle against the Midianites.	*Judges 6:11-24*
Hagar	This former handmaid of Sarah was visited twice by angels: once when she ran away from Sarah's cruelty, once again when she and her son, Ishmael, were driven away from Abraham and Sarah.	*Genesis 16:7-13; 21:15-19*
Hezekiah	An angel of the Lord put to death 185,000 men in the Assyrian camp to bring victory against Sennacherib, king of Assyria.	*2 Kings 19:34-35*
Israelites	Angel sent to the Israelites to warn them of the consequences of their disobedience.	*Judges 2:1-5*
Jacob	Saw an angel of God in a dream about spotted goats. He later struggled with a mysterious man who dislocated his hip and changed Jacob's name to Israel. The man was God himself in the form of an angel.	*Genesis 32:22-32*
Joseph	Saw angels in three dreams of life and death: one to help him decide to marry Mary, the second to get him to take the child to Egypt, and the third with a message of their safety.	*Matthew 1:18-24; 2:13-23*
Lot	Two angels were sent to destroy the cities of Sodom and Gomorrah. Lot and his daughters were saved. His wife was turned into a pillar of salt.	*Genesis 19*
Manoah	An angel appeared first to his wife, who was childless, to tell her she would have a son (Samson). The angel reappeared to Manoah, who saw those words confirmed.	*Judges 13:2-21*

Mary	The angel Gabriel appeared to Mary to announce that she would have a child—Jesus.	Luke 1:26-38
Moses	An "angel of the Lord" appeared to him in a burning bush.	Exodus 3:2–4:10
Paul	While on a ship about to sink, Paul saw an angel with the message that he and the others would be spared.	Acts 27:23-26
Peter	Was freed from prison by an angel.	Acts 12:4-10
Shepherds	First one angel, then a host of angels appeared, proclaiming the birth of the Savior and where he could be found.	Luke 2:8-15
Women	Angel sent to roll back the stone from Jesus' tomb. At the tomb, he told the women that Jesus had risen.	Matthew 28:2-7
Zechariah	The angel Gabriel appeared to Zechariah to announce that he and his wife would have a child in their old age—John the Baptist.	Luke 1:11-20

STRANGE BUT TRUE

The Fourth Man

What mysterious figure joined three condemned prisoners in a roaring furnace?

Soaring flames licked the air surrounding the furnace. They awaited three prisoners destined for an agonizing death. The king, already enraged by the insolence of the men, had commanded it. Despite the fact that the furnace was already hot enough to kill any living thing put inside, King Nebuchadnezzar's voice rang out, "Heat the furnace seven times hotter than usual!" Then he ordered his strongest soldiers to tie up Shadrach, Meshach, and Abednego, the three men standing before him. Bound in heavy rope, they were pushed toward the inferno.

The furnace was so blazing hot that the flames incinerated the soldiers who had thrown the three in. Then King Nebuchadnezzar was on his feet! Frantically he asked his advisors, "Weren't there three men that we tied up and threw into the fire? Look! I see four men walking around, unbound, unharmed, and the fourth looks like a son of the gods!" All of his advisors, shocked with amazement, stared into the fire. Sure enough, not only were the three men walking around in the furnace, but there was a fourth man with them.

Earlier that day, King Nebuchadnezzar had commanded thousands of people to gather in Babylon for the dedication of the golden image. Ninety feet high and nine feet wide, the gigantic idol towered over the people. King Nebuchadnezzar commanded all the peoples and nations of every language to fall down and worship the image of gold. Whoever did not fall down and worship would immediately be thrown into the furnace. Everyone worshiped the idol—except for three men who remained standing amidst the thousands of people gathered on that plain. These three men—Shadrach, Meshach, and Abednego—were Jews whom Nebuchadnezzar had recently appointed as administrators over the entire province of Babylon.

Angry and taken aback, Nebuchadnezzar thought their refusal was simply a misunderstanding. He gave the men a second chance to change their ways, but still they refused. They accepted the likely punishment of death gracefully and added, "If you throw us into the blazing flames, the God we serve is able to save us from it, and he will rescue us. But even if he doesn't, we would never serve your gods or worship the image of gold that you have built!"

And so Nebuchadnezzar hurled the renegades into the furnace. Yet they not only survived, they escaped unharmed.

What happened? When Nebuchadnezzar saw all this and witnessed the fourth man walking in the furnace with the other three, he ordered everyone to worship the God of Shadrach, Meshach, and Abednego.

Yet the question remains: Who was the fourth man? Some Bible scholars say he was probably an angel sent to protect Shadrach, Meshach, and Abednego. Other Bible scholars say he might have been a human manifestation of God himself. In any case, Shadrach, Meshach, and Abednego became lifelong witnesses to the power of the God of Israel.

For more information, read Daniel 3.

FIRESTORMS FROM HEAVEN

Fire pouring down from heaven would be a terrifying sight for any human. Yet such storms happen several times in the pages of Scripture! Where did these firestorms come from? Why did they occur? Here are a few lesser-known cases of this startling—and often deadly—phenomenon.

THE TEMPLE'S FIERY DEDICATION

The magnificent new Temple atop Mount Moriah towered over the city of Jerusalem. King Solomon had dedicated much time, energy, and care in making certain that this building, with all its shining gold, bronze, and silver, was worthy of the Almighty God. Upon its completion, the people of Israel gathered to dedicate the newly constructed house of worship. The occasion was accompanied by lavish feasts and joyful songs. When the first sacrifice was offered, King Solomon stood up and led the people in prayer. When he finished, the entire sky brightened, and a column of fire shot down from heaven and licked up the animal sacrifice that lay on the large, golden altar. In holy fear, the people bowed in worship. (See 2 Chronicles 7:1-4.)

A FIERY GRAVE

The fire that burned up Solomon's sacrifice was one of those rare times when heavenly fire expressed God's pleasure with his servants. Fire from the skies most often destroyed life. Job knew such sorrow firsthand. On one fateful day, he lost most of his family, servants, and livestock to incredible calamities. Some were killed by marauders. His family was killed when the roof of their house caved in. Job also received the tragic news that fire from heaven had burned up his flocks and the servants who tended them. We may conclude from the context of God and Satan's earlier exchange (Job 1:9-12) that Satan himself had called forth the fire. Yet Job refused to blame God for the tragedy. (See Job 1:1-22.)

SATAN'S FIERY END

According to the book of Revelation, firestorms from heaven will mark the end times. Revelation describes a final battle between Satan and God. The wicked will gather around Satan to form a terrifying army. Satan's evil hordes will surround God's people, preparing themselves for the final deadly assault. But at the last moment, Satan's entire army will be wiped out with a hot, fiery blast from heaven. The defeat leads to Satan's everlasting torment in the Lake of Fire and to the victory of God's people. (See Revelation 20:9-10.)

DID YOU KNOW?

What is the pillar of fire?

The Israelites who fled from Egypt to their Promised Land witnessed many wonders. Perhaps most memorable were the manna that rained down from heaven (Exodus 16:31) and the water that gushed from a rock (Exodus 17:1-7). The most mystifying phenomenon, however, was the pillar of fire that guided the Israelites at night (Exodus 13:21-22). Some have wondered whether the pillar of fire described in the Bible was actually volcanic eruptions in the Sinai region. But the descriptions of the pillar of fire seem to preclude such an explanation. How could a volcanic eruption shine light on the Israelites but at the same time cover the Egyptians in darkness (Exodus 14:19-20)? In the end, no one can offer a natural explanation for the column of fire that followed the Israelite camp during those 40 years in the desert. But it is clear from the Bible that the fiery pillar represented God and his holiness. It was both a brilliant light that provided physical safety and a luminous reminder of the source of all spiritual enlightenment.

The Shadows of the Crucifixion

What explains the phenomena that surrounded Jesus' death?

The radical rabbi from Nazareth hung from a Roman crossbeam between two common criminals. A crowd of the curious and a handful of Jesus' closest friends watched from a distance. As the controversial teacher slowly died, people in various parts of Jerusalem went about their pre-Sabbath rituals, trying to make sense of what appeared to be a chain of seemingly unrelated circumstances.

From noon to three o'clock that dreadful Friday, the sky was ominously dark. At first it was thought to be a total eclipse of the sun. But when it continued longer than an hour, other explanations were sought. At about three o'clock that afternoon, a light earthquake rumbled beneath the ground. Some of the more insecure buildings in Jerusalem and the surrounding villages toppled. Panicked children ran from their places of play to the safety of their parents. The priests gathered at the Temple for afternoon prayers could be heard screaming. The thick woven veil that hung from the pillared heights of the Temple and separated the holy place from the Most Holy Place ripped in two. What was especially curious was the fact that the veil tore from top to bottom.

Reports began to circulate around the city that a number of tombstones had rolled away from the entrance to the aboveground burial caves. Reports circulated that individuals who had been long dead and buried were seen walking around the streets of Jerusalem. Something strange was going on. But no one could put a finger on the cause of all the commotion.

Wouldn't it be realistic to think that the earthquake was the common thread of all the unusual activity that was being reported? The dark sky was probably some meteorological portent of the collision of intercontinental plates under the ground. And the earthquake could have caused the Temple veil to tear. An earthquake would have the power to unseal gravestones. And the fear engendered by such a turbulent event would cause people to act hysterically and think they were seeing people they really weren't—like dead people walking.

But what if the events didn't hinge on an earthquake? What if the earthquake was simply a consequence of some greater cataclysmic occurrence? What if all the strange happenings of this unforgettable Friday were connected to the public execution going on outside the city limits? A centurion soldier, who stood at the base of the cross on which the rabbi Jesus hung, wouldn't have been surprised if that were the case. He couldn't help but wonder about the person he stood watching. This was no ordinary criminal on this cross and he knew it. And this was no ordinary afternoon.

But what if the seemingly insignificant rabbi was not insignificant? What if he was who he claimed to be? If he in fact was the Son of God, would not his death result in some supernatural consequences?

Draw your own conclusions about what happened that day. Start with Matthew 27 and Mark 15.

CURIOUS CONNECTIONS

GOD'S MOUNTAIN

Although no one today is completely certain of its location, there is a place mentioned in both the Old and New Testaments of the Bible as Mount Sinai. Sometimes called Mount Horeb, this site is so important that it is referred to in some translations as "God's mountain," and for good reason. This holy site figured time and again in Israel's spiritual history.

THE BURNING BUSH THAT DID NOT BURN

Moses, who later became the great prophet of the Israelite people, was tending sheep in the desert of Sinai. While he was there, he saw a bush that was on fire but did not burn up. Fascinated, he approached to investigate. Imagine his surprise and fright when he heard a voice coming from the bush. Not just any voice, but the voice of the living God! Moses obeyed God's command to remove his sandals, for the mountainside he stood on was God's holy ground.

Moses discovered then that he had been chosen to lead God's people from Egypt. (See Exodus 3:1-22.)

IN THE PRESENCE OF GOD
After the prophet Moses led the Israelite people out of slavery in Egypt, he took them to Mount Sinai as God had instructed. Leaving the people camped at the base of the mountain, Moses scaled its heights to speak with and worship God. Yahweh descended to the mountain in a bright cloud and gave his law to Moses. Afterward, when Moses returned, the people noticed that his face was shining brightly because he had been in the presence of God. The tablets he carried with him contained a summary of the law for Israel, often called the Ten Commandments. (See Exodus 34:1-35.)

SANCTUARY
Having just experienced a tremendous victory over the priests of Baal, the Israelite prophet Elijah found himself on the run for his life. Jezebel, queen of Israel, had demanded his death for his humiliation of her priests. An angel told him to journey hundreds of miles to Mount Sinai. At Sinai, we are told, God came to him and asked why he was there. Elijah told God his troubles, and God responded by telling the prophet to go stand out on the mountain so that Elijah could see him when God passed by. Then a strong wind shook the mountain and shattered the rocks. It was followed by an earthquake, then a fire. But God did not reveal his presence until he spoke in the whisper of a gentle breeze. Reassured, Elijah followed God's instructions and returned the way he had come. (See 1 Kings 19:1-18.)

POSTRESURRECTION APPEARANCES OF JESUS

The New Testament begins and ends with the salvation epic of Jesus of Nazareth. But the biblical record includes more than his birth, his ministry, and his death. Because he rose from the grave, his message continues to affect lives today. Here are the witnesses who saw Jesus after his death and proclaimed the news that he still lives today.

1. Two women named Mary saw him when they hurried away from his tomb (Matthew 28:1-10; John 20:10-18).
2. Eleven of his disciples saw him on a mountain in Galilee (Matthew 28:16-20).
3. Mary Magdalene saw him on Easter morning (Mark 16:9).
4. Two people met him, walking in the country on the road to Emmaus (Mark 16:12-19; Luke 24:13-32).
5. Ten of his disciples saw him in the city of Jerusalem (Luke 24:36-51; John 20:19-23).
6. The disciple Thomas, who had not been with the rest when Jesus appeared to them in Jerusalem, touched his scars (John 20:24-31).
7. His disciples saw him by the sea and had breakfast with him (John 21:1-25).
8. His disciples saw him before he rose into heaven (Acts 1:3-9).
9. Saul (later called Paul) encountered Jesus on the road to Damascus (Acts 9:1-6).
10. The elderly disciple John received a grand vision from Jesus on the island of Patmos (Revelation 1).

STRANGE BUT TRUE

Fire from the Sky

A bold prophet triumphs over a pagan cult

The lifeless bodies of pagan priests were randomly piled at the base of Israel's famed Mount Carmel. A day of challenge was now complete. Baal's prophets had lost. A solitary prophet of God named Elijah had been vindicated. But how had it happened? Only hours before on top of the mountain, thousands had gathered at the king's invitation to witness the duel of the century: Elijah against 450 prophets of Baal.

Elijah's challenge was simple. An offering would be presented to each deity—to Baal and to the God of Israel. Each offering was to be burned on an altar. There was only one catch: Flint starters and torches were prohibited. The fire to consume the sacrifice had to come from the respective deities. The scenario seemed impossible. Yet each side agreed to the terms of the challenge.

As the people gathered, there was excitement in the air. But watching the Baal prophets spend hour after hour imploring and pleading with Baal soon grew old. No matter how carefully they recited their ritual, no matter how passionately they shouted, no matter how fiercely they slashed themselves, nothing happened. Nothing. The sun passed high over head, and nothing happened. The only thrill of the entire afternoon was Elijah's loud taunt: "Pray louder; maybe Baal is asleep." The afternoon sun began to fade on the horizon; still, nothing happened. The exhausted and embarrassed challengers one by one gave up.

It was Elijah's turn. His simple stone altar sat ready. At Elijah's command, the butchered animal was drenched with cool, sparkling water. After the entire altar was thoroughly soaked, Elijah called out to Israel's God. Suddenly a deafening roar filled the air. Red-hot fire rained down from heaven. The sacrifice, the stone altar, and the ground around it were consumed in one breathtaking instant. All that was left was a blackened heap. The wide-eyed spectators stared at it in amazement.

What happened that day? Was this a case of spontaneous combustion? Not likely. There would have been little chance that water-logged lumber would spontaneously burst into flames. Could it have been a lightning strike? Lightning would surely have caused a fire, but it wouldn't have consumed the very stones of the altar. Moreover, there wasn't a cloud in the sky. The land had been suffering a drought for months.

The spectators were certainly convinced that only God could produce such a firestorm. The dead bodies of the Baal prophets were a sign of the prophets' lies and their complete rejection of God. The Almighty was the only one capable of such a fiery feat.

To learn more about this spectacular event for yourself, read 1 Kings 18.

LAKES, OCEANS, RIVERS, AND WATERS

Oceans, rivers, and lakes were mysterious, foreboding, and daunting in Bible times. Their power and danger were respected, and they often became the scene for miracles and other unusual occurrences.

Occurrence	Reference
God once punished the Egyptians by causing all the fish in the Nile River to die, making it smell so foul that the people could not drink its water.	*Exodus 7:21*
God allowed the sea to part so that the Israelites could cross, but closed it over Pharaoh and his Egyptian armies when they followed behind. Pharaoh and his armies were drowned.	*Exodus 15:4*
God commanded Moses to strike a rock twice with a stick. When he did, water gushed out—enough for all the people and animals to drink.	*Numbers 20:11*
The Levites carried the Ark into the Jordan, and the water parted, allowing the people to cross to the other side.	*Joshua 3:16*
God provided a spring to refresh the exhausted Samson.	*Judges 15:19*
Elijah struck a river with his cloak, and the water parted.	*2 Kings 2:8*
Elisha healed the waters of a polluted spring.	*2 Kings 2:21*
Elisha told Jehoshaphat that he would be able to water his flocks in the midst of drought. The next day, the valley was filled with water.	*2 Kings 3:17-20*
When Naaman washed in the Jordan River seven times, he was completely healed of his leprosy.	*2 Kings 5:10*
The prophet Daniel once had a dream where he saw a river of fire.	*Daniel 7:10*
During a fierce storm, the prophet Jonah told his ship-mates to throw him into the sea. When they did, the storm stopped immediately.	*Jonah 1:12-15*
Jesus was baptized in the Jordan, and the Spirit descended on him in the form of a dove.	*Matthew 3:16*

When Jesus' disciples saw him walking on the water, they were terrified, thinking he was a ghost.		*Matthew 14:25-26*
Possessed by demons, a herd of 2,000 pigs rushed down a steep bank and into a lake where they drowned.		*Mark 5:13*
The apostle Paul listed flooded rivers and stormy seas among the most grave dangers he had faced.		*2 Corinthians 11:26*
The book of Revelation tells of a sea that looks like crystal-clear glass.		*Revelation 4:6*
The serpent's mouth gushed a flood of water like a river, which swept a woman away. But the earth swallowed the flood, saving her.		*Revelation 12:15-16*
An angel pours out a bowl into the oceans, and they all become like blood, killing everything in them.		*Revelation 16:3*
The Lake of Fire, mentioned in the Bible, is composed of burning sulfur.		*Revelation 19:20*
After the present earth is destroyed there will be a new earth, and it will have no oceans.		*Revelation 21:1*

STORMS AND WEIRD WEATHER

Thunder, lightning, rushing wind—God used all of these signs to show his power to the world. Here is a summary of a few extraordinary weather events and a theological explanation of why they happened.

Weather or Atmospheric Condition	What Happened	Reference
Torrential rain	God sent torrential rain for 40 days and 40 nights, covering the earth with water for 150 days and blotting out all life. Only Noah and his family survived.	*Genesis 7:10-24*

Rainbow	God set a rainbow in the clouds for the first time to promise that he would never again destroy the earth with a flood.	*Genesis 9:12-17*
Wind	After the Lord miraculously parted the Red Sea, a strong wind blew all night to dry the sea floor so Moses and the people could cross on dry ground.	*Exodus 14:21-22*
Strange dew	In Israel's camp, dew covered the ground in the morning. When it dried, it turned into white flakes that tasted like honey bread. The people of Israel ate this food, called manna, for 40 years!	*Exodus 16:13-35*
Raining quails	The Lord caused a huge wind, which picked up thousands of quails from the sea and dropped them into the camp where Moses and the people were staying.	*Numbers 11:31-33*
Earthquake	The earth split in two and swallowed up 250 people who were rebelling against God. They fell into the grave, and the earth closed back over them.	*Numbers 16:31-33*
Hail	As the enemy was fleeing during one of Joshua's battles, God caused a hailstorm. More men were killed by the falling hailstones than had been killed in the entire battle.	*Joshua 10:11*
Fixed sun	Because of Joshua's prayer, the sun stood still in the sky, allowing Joshua to completely destroy a pagan army.	*Joshua 10:12-14*

Strange-shaped cloud	After praying for rain, the prophet Elijah saw a cloud that looked about the size of a man's hand rising from the sea. A torrential rainstorm followed.	*1 Kings 18:41-45*
Destructive wind	A strong wind from the desert collapsed the roof of a house, killing all of Job's children.	*Job 1:18-19*
Whirlwind	God talked to Job from inside a great whirlwind.	*Job 38:1*
Bright star	A star guided the wise men and others thousands of miles to where Jesus was born in Bethlehem.	*Matthew 2:2*
Terrible storm	High waves and a strong windstorm rocked the disciples' boat, making them terribly afraid for their lives. But when Jesus rebuked the storm, it stopped, and all was calm.	*Matthew 8:23-27*
Earthquake	The whole earth was covered in darkness for three hours before Jesus died on the cross. A powerful earthquake rocked Jerusalem, the curtain in the Temple was split from top to bottom, and graves opened when he died.	*Matthew 27:51-53*
Earthquake	A strong earthquake caused a prison's doors to fly wide open and prisoners' chains to fall off, including those of Paul and Silas.	*Acts 16:25-27*

Shipwreck

A prisoner foresees a terrible shipwreck and the survival of all on board

As the ferocity of the winds increased, Julius glanced anxiously at the prisoners in the hull. If the winds got any worse, there was a real chance of shipwreck! How would he, the centurion and highest ranking official on board, prevent any of the prisoners from swimming away and escaping? The sailors were scurrying around, frantically throwing cargo overboard, securing the lifeboat, and even passing ropes under the ship to hold it together. Raging, the hurricane whipped the boat from side to side. Julius was now more concerned with his own life.

As a last resort, the sailors threw the ship's tackle overboard. Without seeing the sun or stars for days, everyone aboard gave up all hope of being saved.

But then one of the prisoners, a man named Paul, stood up and told the men on board about a strange dream he had. The centurion Julius could hardly believe what Paul said: "Not one of you will be lost! Keep up your courage for only the ship will be destroyed. Last night, an angel of the God I serve told me that God has graciously given me the lives of all of you—so don't be afraid!" Julius laughed to himself. How could the ship be destroyed, and yet not one of them would die? But if this man was telling the truth, did he mean the prisoners as well? Surely they would try to escape.

After 14 days, as the storm drove the tiny ship across the raging Adriatic Sea, the experienced sailors sensed that land was drawing near. Fearing they would be dashed against the rocks of an island or coral reef, some let down a lifeboat in a desperate attempt to escape. Paul stopped them, telling Julius that the men would certainly die if they left the ship. For some reason, Julius believed this man—this awkward and visionary prisoner who was so different from the others. The centurion ordered the soldiers on board and cut the lifeboat free.

Just as Paul had predicted, the ship struck a sandbar. The stern was broken to pieces by the pounding surf. Before the soldiers made their way to the safety of the island shores, they determined that they should kill all the prisoners, including Paul. If any got away, the soldiers would pay with their own lives—something not one of them wanted to do. But Julius interceded. Paul, although a prisoner, had already proven himself useful.

Remarkably, everyone got to land, saved from the ferocious seas, just as Paul had foretold. Who was this man? How could he foresee the future? These were only some of the questions that plagued the soldiers and sailors who accompanied Paul.

But the surprises didn't end with Paul's prediction. Once on shore, Paul was bitten by a poisonous snake. In ancient times, this usually led to instant death. But for Paul, it meant nothing. Unaffected by poisonous snakes, he continued to tell the people about his great message of Good News. Now, the islanders were nothing less than astonished. Who was this man? What kind of prophet could he be?

For more information about Paul's adventures, read Acts 27–28.

STRANGE BUT TRUE

Mountaintop Encounter

Who stood with Jesus during the Transfiguration?

As the sun blazed down on them, Peter, James, and John followed Jesus up the rugged path to the very top of the mountain. From such heights, they could look far below on the few shepherds who gathered their flocks together in the barren valley. Jesus had come to this distant place to pray. He withdrew to a solitary place to concentrate in prayer. The disciples, exhausted from the trip, fell down to rest.

Within seconds, Jesus' appearance seemed to get brighter and brighter. It quickly became unmistakable. Jesus was dazzling white now. His face glowed; his appearance had completely changed. Suddenly two bright beings, as dazzling white as Jesus was, appeared next to Jesus. They were humans but in some different, brilliant form. They conversed with Jesus for a while. And then a brilliant cloud shone over the entire mountaintop. From the cloud, a voice thundered: "This is my beloved Son. Listen to him." Then in an instant, the apparitions disappeared, just as quickly as they had appeared. Jesus was left as he had been before—in a white, dusty robe.

Are ghosts for real? Do people from the past live in a different dimension and return to earth for special visits, like in ghost stories?

At least in the case of these beings—later identified by the disciples as Elijah and Moses—it appears they do. This was no video replay in ancient times; the disciples witnessed this incident on an ordinary day about 2,000 years ago. The disciples believed in a spiritual life that extends beyond physical death, but they had never seen anything like this. That heavenly life that Moses and Elijah exhibited most certainly takes on a different form than the three-dimensional one we are accustomed to. Yet the similarities are striking. They looked like human beings to the stunned disciples. But the differences are even more striking. The disciples could not begin to understand or even describe the mechanics of life in other dimensions. It was beyond their comprehension just as it is ours. They could only describe those heavenly life forms as wonderful and magnificent. Even those words are too small to describe it.

Do people from the past visit this earth often, as Moses and Elijah did on that day? Scripture indicates that this was a special manifestation of heavenly glories for the disciples' benefit. Yet the author of Hebrews reminds us that we sometimes entertain angels without recognizing them (Hebrews 13:2). At least the mysterious apparitions on the mountaintop point to an interesting possibility— life of another quality, pure and bright.

To read about the disciples' encounter with heavenly beings, turn to Matthew 17 or Mark 9.

ANGELS

Do angels really exist?

Most of us haven't seen an angel and, in this life, probably never will. Does that mean angels do not exist? Some have answered this question with a resounding yes. For these people, seeing is believing. For them, human experience defines reality. But many people, including those mentioned in the Bible, know that reality cannot be limited to the narrow confines of human experience. There is a supernatural world, a world that exists beyond space and time. God occupies this world because he is a Spirit (John 4:24). But he has also created spiritual beings called angels. These beings are his messengers. The Bible describes angels appearing to all sorts of people—from Gideon to Mary, from Samson's father and mother to Balaam and his donkey (Numbers 22:21-35; Judges 6:12-24; 13:2-24; Luke 1:26-38). These angels left a host of startled people and changed lives behind as evidence of their comings and goings.

Do people have guardian angels?

God has assigned some angels to stand watch over those who trust in the Lord (Psalm 34:7; 91:11). The Bible, however, doesn't say that every individual is assigned an angel. Jesus did say that there were angels who watched over children (Matthew 18:10). But it was Jewish tradition that taught that people had a guardian angel who looked like the person that angel was assigned to. The Christians who gathered to pray at Mary's house may have been expressing that Jewish belief when they told the girl who claimed she saw Peter that she had probably seen Peter's angel. (See Acts 12:15.)

Why doesn't God just appear to people? Why does he send angels?

The Bible says that no one has seen God (John 1:18; 1 John 4:20). No one can see God because he lives in unapproachable light (1 Timothy 6:16). Anyone who does see God will die

(Exodus 33:20; Judges 13:21-22). Because of this chasm between humans and God, the Lord uses angels as messengers. He usually sends angels when he wants to impress on a person that the message is a direct order from God himself (see Gideon's experience in Judges 6:11-27).

Is there any common experience that people who were visited by angels share?

The Bible records a number of incidents when people have encountered angels (Genesis 16:7; 19:1; 28:12; Exodus 3:2). The one common response of all these people is utter fear. The guards at Jesus' tomb shook in fear when a shining angel appeared (Matthew 28:4). Cornelius, a Roman centurion, stared at an angel with sheer terror (Acts 10:2-4). Zechariah was frightened when an angel appeared to him in the Temple (Luke 1:11). These people were justifiably afraid, for angels are God's servants empowered to do his will on this earth. Those who insist on opposing God's will can only expect to face an angel's sharp sword of punishment, as Balaam did (Numbers 22:23-34) and other enemies of God did (2 Kings 19:35). It is only when an angel says, "Do not be afraid," that a person knows for certain that the message the angel bears is one of peace, not judgment (Luke 1:13, 30).

SIX

PERPLEXING PROPHECIES

Strange Predictions and Shocking Curses

Balaam and the Beast

Directives from heaven come from an animal's mouth

As King Balak looked out over the Jordan River, he could see Israelites covering the landscape as far as he could see. He trembled in fear. Balak, the king of Moab, was terrified of the Israelites because of news that he had recently received. King Sihon's people, the Amorites, and King Og's people of Bashan had been wiped from the face of the earth. The Israelites had utterly destroyed them; there wasn't a single survivor.

And now these same Israelites were camped along the Jordan, too close to his own people. Fighting the Israelites did not seem to work so well; they were too powerful. Balak wondered what else might work. The Israelites would certainly want his land as well. And so he decided to put a curse on them. He wanted all the help he could get. Perhaps the curse of an old prophet would weaken them in order to give him victory!

Balak knew of a man named Balaam. Some people called him a prophet, and some called him a sorcerer. All Balak knew was that Balaam seemed to have magical powers. Whomever Balaam blessed seemed to do extraordinarily well. Whomever he cursed was doomed. It was only a matter of time. Balak had to get this man to curse the Israelites. So he sent his elders, along with a great deal of money, to get Balaam and bring him to this spot to place a curse on these invaders.

Several days later, the elders of Moab returned—*without* Balaam. Balak couldn't believe it! So he sent other men, more distinguished than the first group, to persuade this old prophet to come. Along with them, he sent a message to Balaam: "Do not let anything keep you from coming to me, because I will reward you handsomely and do whatever you say. Come and curse these people!" This time, Balaam came. However, Balak was angry at the delay and therefore did not notice Balaam's odd behavior.

Balak brought the distinguished old prophet to a high point looking down over the vast Israelite camp below. Balak waited expectantly to hear the curse, the curse that would doom this people. But as Balaam opened his mouth, only words of blessing came out. Balak couldn't believe his ears. "What have you done to me?" he cried out. But Balak would not give up.

Balak took Balaam to another high point that looked over the Israelites. Once again, as soon as Balaam opened his mouth, words of blessing poured out. A third time, from another spot, Balaam blessed the Israelites—except this time he cursed Moab also! Balak, filled with anger and completely confused, was furious with Balaam. What was he doing? But every time Balak rebuked the old prophet, Balaam responded, "Must I not speak what the Lord puts in my mouth?"

What had gotten into this loyal and old prophet of Canaan? Balak couldn't even guess, but Balaam started to tell a bizarre tale, one Balak didn't know whether to believe.

Apparently, Balaam had been on his way to curse the Israelites, when his loyal donkey began behaving very strangely. The donkey veered off the path into a nearby field, crushed Balaam's foot against the wall of a vineyard, and even lay down in the middle of the road. Donkeys are known for being stubborn, but Balaam's donkey had never done anything like this before! All three times, Balaam did what any owner would do to a disobedient donkey; he beat it again and again to get it moving. But as he was beating the animal a third time, Balaam said he couldn't believe his own ears. His donkey started talking to him in a raspy but audible voice. "What have I done to you to make you beat me three times?"

Balaam was dumbfounded! A donkey . . . talking? But then he

saw something even stranger: a terrifying angel with a brilliant sword. His words sounded like a thunderclap. "Go to Moab, but say only what I tell you."

Balak didn't know whether to believe Balaam's strange story. But he did know Balaam was acting strange. Balaam would always curse those he told him to curse. Why wouldn't he do the same for the Israelites? It didn't make sense. Maybe Balaam's tale of a sword-laden angel was true. What else was protecting these Israelites from King Sihon and King Og?

As it turned out, Balak could have saved himself from all that speculation. Like the kings before him, Balak was routed by the Israelites.

For more information, read Numbers 21–23.

CURIOUS CONNECTIONS

MIRACULOUS BIRTHS

The birth of a baby is a small miracle. While the parents may stare starry-eyed at the miracle of new life, the rest of the world bustles on as if nothing spectacular happened. Babies are born every day—but not to a 100-year-old woman, a barren woman, or even a virgin. Such births are extraordinary occurrences that inspire wonder and awe.

ISAAC

Abraham and his wife, Sarah, were well advanced in their years, and Sarah was way past the age of childbearing. Yet at the age of 100, Abraham fathered a son! One day, three strange visitors in shining white came to Abraham and Sarah's tent as they were resting during the heat of the day. After Abraham and Sarah prepared food for them, one of the visitors told Abraham an unbelievable thing. He said that within one year Sarah would have a son. *Ha!* thought Sarah, *at my age?* But as she laughed at the idea, the visitor said, "Is anything too hard for the Lord?" One year later, at the age of 90, Sarah gave birth to Isaac, the inheritor of Abraham's covenant. (See Genesis 18:1-15; 21:1-7.)

JOHN THE BAPTIST

Zechariah and his wife, Elizabeth, were childless. Not only were they well along in years, but Elizabeth was also barren. One day when Zechariah, a priest, was in the Temple, a stranger appeared by the altar. The stranger called himself Gabriel, an angel of the God of Israel. Gabriel told Zechariah that his wife would bear a son. Zechariah was to name the son John and dedicate the child's life to God. This child was to follow in the footsteps of the great prophet Elijah. Zechariah could not believe his ears and questioned the angel. Because he doubted the news, Gabriel said he would be struck dumb until the baby was born. Immediately Zechariah lost his ability to speak. But when a son was born to the once-barren Elizabeth in her old age, Zechariah's mouth was opened. The child became known as John the Baptist, a great prophet who prophesied Jesus' coming. (See Luke 1:5-25, 57-80; 3:1-18.)

JESUS

Mary, a virgin, was startled by a bright light. When she turned around, a stranger who called himself Gabriel, an angel of the God of Israel, was standing before her. He told her that she was to give birth to a son. She was to name the son Jesus, and he would be known as the Son of God. "How can I have a baby? I am a virgin," Mary asked. Gabriel replied, "The Holy Spirit will come upon you. . . . Nothing is impossible with God." There was no union between Mary and any man, and yet she gave birth to a son nine months after Gabriel appeared to her. Her son was called Jesus. (See Matthew 1:18-25; Luke 1:26-38.)

STRANGE BUT TRUE

A Curse for the Tyrant

A survivor of a massacre predicts the downfall of a murderous ruler

Through the smoky haze, the woman in the tower kept her eyes on Abimelech below. He and his men had just besieged and captured the city. So all the people of the city had fled into the tower, locked themselves in, and climbed onto the roof. But as Abimelech and his men approached the tall tower to storm it, he was stopped dead in his tracks. His servant, close beside him, could not believe what had just happened. The woman from the tower had dropped a millstone, a round stone used for grinding grain. The stone fell in the right place and the right time. It struck Abimelech directly, crushing his skull.

With his last breath, Abimelech whispered to his servant to kill him with his sword, so he would die honorably as a soldier—not by the hands of a woman. Abimelech, king of Israel and ruler of the citizens of Shechem, was dead! "It's Jotham's curse!" one Israelite yelled, when he heard the citizens talking about the horrific and sudden death of Abimelech. All the people of the region had been wondering whether or not Jotham's curse, made three years earlier, would actually come true. Abimelech was their king! Yet, within three years, he had torn apart his nation with battles upon battles. Now he was dead, the victim of a freak incident.

Under Abimelech's reign, a terrible mass execution had occurred. Seventy brothers were murdered, and the blood of these men, Gideon's sons, was mingled together in their home at Ophrah. Abimelech, a son of Gideon and his concubine, ruthlessly killed all but one of his half brothers. Jotham, the youngest brother and the only one to escape, witnessed every gory detail. He could still hear his brothers' haunting screams echoing throughout the countryside. How could Abimelech, son of his father's slave girl, do this? Fresh blood was stilling drying on the rocks of the murder scene, when miles away, the citizens of Shechem and Beth-millo gathered to crown Abimelech king!

News of Abimelech's victory over the sons of Gideon had spread throughout Shechem. The people gathered to acknowledge his strength and cleverness. He would be a great king for Israel, everyone thought. No one could match his power. But on that fateful day, a voice rang out from Mount Gerizim. It was Jotham, the last of Gideon's sons. With anger and bitterness, Jotham placed a curse on Abimelech and the citizens of Shechem.

"If you have acted honorably and in good faith toward Gideon and his family today, may Abimelech be your joy, and may you be his, too! But if you have not, let fire come out from Abimelech and consume you, citizens of Shechem, and let fire come out from you, citizens of Shechem, and consume Abimelech!" Three years later, the city was destroyed by fire, and Abimelech lay dead. Was this a mere coincidence or divine justice? Was this a tragic set of unrelated events or a fulfillment of a curse placed on Abimelech's head three years earlier? The last statement about Abimelech in the book of Judges seems to leave no room for debate: "So the curse of Jotham son of Gideon came true."

Abimelech's short and cruel reign ended, and Israel gained a new ruler, Tola, from the tribe of Issachar.

For more information on Jotham's curse and the violent life of Abimelech, read Judges 9.

CURIOUS CONNECTIONS

BINDING CURSES
Many people today flippantly curse everything—from a passing motorist to even a close friend. Not many people think twice about it. But the ancients knew that words should not be spoken so lightly. Words are binding. Words cannot be taken back once they have been spoken. Curses can have as much power as the awful deeds they invoke. The following stories relate the power of curses on the lives of people in the Bible.

THE CURSE OF THE GARDEN
Everything was perfect when Adam and Eve started their life together in Paradise. They lived in the beautiful Garden of Eden. But their idyllic existence was disrupted by one simple act: a bite from the fruit of the tree of knowledge. Adam and Eve ate and took upon themselves a curse that would plague them and all their descendants. God told them that the land would bear a curse of thorns, and the man would have to sweat long hours to obtain food to eat. The woman was also cursed. She would suffer pain in childbirth. And both Adam and Eve would die (Genesis 3:14-19). Their sinful act was irreversible, and so was the curse. Women still suffer great pain

BLESSINGS

God's people have been asking for and giving blessings since the first generations walked the earth. Here are but a few of the biblical blessings . . . and their sometimes unusual results.

Blesser	Circumstances or Results	Reference
Melchizedek, priest and the king of Jerusalem	Abram, whose devotion to God increased and who then gave a tenth of his possessions to Melchizedek	Genesis 14:17-20
God	Noah and his sons; God established a covenant with them after the flood	Genesis 9:1-11
Isaac	Jacob steals his brother Esau's blessing from their father; years of sibling rivalry result	Genesis 27:1-40
Moses	Israelites; they had set up the Tabernacle exactly as God had commanded	Exodus 39:42-43
God	Job; the last part of his life—after all his trials—had more abundance and joy than the first part	Job 42:12-17
God	Person who follows God's ways; grows and prospers	Psalm 1
God	Several rather surprising kinds of people, such as the meek, the pure in spirit, mourners, the insulted; according to Jesus, they receive various blessings	Matthew 5:1-12
Christians	Other people; those who bless instead of insulting or repaying evil with evil will in turn inherit a blessing from God	1 Peter 3:8-14
The Lamb on the throne (Jesus)	He is on the throne in heaven, being worshiped by all creation	Revelation 5

in childbirth today, and every person born on this earth can expect to die.

AND THE VERDICT IS...

The ancient Israelites had an elaborate procedure for jealous husbands to use if they suspected their wives of adultery. A suspicious husband could bring his wife to a priest. After making a mixture of dirt and water, the priest would speak an oath that acquitted the woman if innocent or condemned her if guilty. The woman was then required to say, "Yes, let it be so" and drink the water. If the water made her sick, she was presumed guilty. The liquid would render her childless for the rest of her life. Her name would become a curse among the people. (See Numbers 5:11-31.)

LIES, ALL LIES!

The Israelites were victorious everywhere they went. The cities of Jericho and Ai had fallen to Israel's triumphant army, and the news of this spread fast. The people of the city of Gibeon were terrified. They knew that they had no chance against the invading Israelites. So they sent a delegation to the Israelites disguised as travelers from a distant land. This deceitful delegation approached Joshua with a humble request: a peace treaty. Joshua, believing them to be from a region beyond what Israel had determined to conquer, fell for the trick and signed a peace treaty with them. But when he learned the truth later, he vehemently cursed them. He condemned them to chopping wood and carrying water for the Israelites, a curse that literally came to pass. (See Joshua 9:3-27.)

DID YOU KNOW?

How did a prophet know the name of the man who would order the exiles to return to Jerusalem?

Isaiah was an extraordinary prophet—a man who had seen the throne room of heaven, who had commanded a shadow to move backwards, and who had paraded naked for three years as a prophetic sign (2 Kings 20:8-11; Isaiah 6:1-13; 20:1-5). Isaiah prophesied from around 740 B.C. to 681 B.C., but his predictions encompassed all of human history. He predicted Jerusalem's destruction 100 years before it happened and the rebuilding of the Temple 200 years before it occurred. The most intriguing prophecy is the one involving Cyrus: 150 years before Cyrus reigned as king of Persia (559–530 B.C.), Isaiah predicted that a man named Cyrus would rule many kings and would order the Israelites to rebuild Jerusalem and the Temple, which actually happened in March of 538 B.C. (compare Isaiah 44:28 with Ezra 1:1-4). Jewish tradition claims that Cyrus read Isaiah's prophecy and was astonished with the resemblance to his life.

STRANGE BUT TRUE

Jephthah's Vow

Would an Israelite kill his only daughter?

As the door of his house opened, Jephthah's face froze in horror. His only daughter was rushing out to greet him, dancing with a tambourine in her hand. At that moment, he realized what a terrible thing he had done—he was going to have to kill his only daughter. Jephthah cried out in anguish, "My daughter! My heart is breaking! What a tragedy that you came out to greet me! For I have made a vow to the Lord and cannot take it back." What kind of vow had he made?

Early that morning, Jephthah, a great warrior and a judge for the Israelites, made a vow to the God of Israel. He was about to lead his army against the Ammonite nation, and he asked God to give him victory that day. Jephthah promised that he would give God the first thing that came out of his house to greet him when he returned in triumph. He vowed to sacrifice whatever it was as a burnt offering. The God of Israel had commanded the Israelites that when a man makes a vow he must not break his word. Consequently, it seems obvious that Jephthah sacrificed his only daughter as a burnt offering to God. But ambiguity remains . . .

Sacrificing children to pagan gods is part of the ugly record of some ancient religions. In fact, the Ammonites sacrificed their children to the god Molech to appease their vengeful deity. The God of the Israelites, on the other hand, abhorred human sacrifice. God explicitly forbade the practice of human sacrifice in his list of instructions for the Israelite nation (Leviticus 18:21). In Genesis, God used the concept of human sacrifice to test Abraham. God asked Abraham to sacrifice his only and long-awaited son, Isaac. However, God was testing Abraham's faith and obedience. He stopped Abraham from carrying through with the sacrifice.

So why would the God of Israel, a God of love and mercy, accept Jephthah's vow? Did Jephthah really sacrifice his only daughter as a burnt offering? Surprisingly, his daughter's reaction to the vow was not anger or fear. She replied, "Father, you have made a promise to the Lord. You must do to me what you have promised, for the Lord has given you a great victory over your enemies, the Ammonites. But first, let me go up and roam in the hills and weep with my friends for two months, because I will die a virgin."

The Bible says Jephthah did to her as he had vowed. She died a virgin.

However, even scholars are divided over whether or not his daughter was sacrificed. The God of Israel could not possibly have honored a vow based on a wicked practice. Perhaps she was set aside as a virgin for the rest of her life, which in essence meant death for the family, because there would be no children to carry on Jephthah's name. And why would she leave for two months if the whole point behind the sacrifice was immediate rejoicing and thanksgiving for Jephthah's victory?

For more information, see Judges 11 and Genesis 22.

CURIOUS CONNECTIONS

A THROW OF THE DICE

Dice thrown, lots cast—decisions were often made by games of chance. The ancients believed that divine guidance, not luck, would determine the outcome. Besides the Urim and Thummin, the mysterious stones that the priest of Israel consulted, lots and dice often shaped the destiny of ancient Israel and even that of the early church.

AND THE WINNER IS . . .

After the Israelites had captured vast tracts of territory in Canaan, they had to divide the land among the 12 tribes. Five of the tribes had been given sections of land that became their inheritance, but the remaining land had yet to be divided by the other seven tribes. Their leader, Joshua, left that decision in God's hands. At Shiloh, the resting place of the Tabernacle, Joshua ordered that the remaining land be surveyed, then divided by the casting of sacred lots. In this way each tribe gained its inheritance. (See Joshua 18:1-10.)

AND THE GUILTY PARTY IS . . .

Saul, the first king of the Israelites, wanted to destroy the Philistine army by pursuing them in an all-night chase. At the suggestion of his priest, Saul cast lots to determine if this course was wise. But the lots gave him no answer, so Saul knew that something was wrong. He cast lots again to determine the source of the sin. The results pointed to his own son, Jonathan, who had tasted honey despite Saul's order to the army that they fast until the enemy was defeated. Saul was prepared to execute Jonathan, but the people of Israel persuaded him not to because of Jonathan's heroism in battle. (See 1 Samuel 14:36-45.)

YOU CAN RUN BUT YOU CAN'T HIDE

Jonah had received orders from God—orders that he did not want to follow. He tried to run by getting on a ship and sailing away. A great storm sprang up and threatened to destroy the ship. The sailors were frightened and wanted to know who was causing their misfortune. They cast lots and discovered that Jonah had angered the gods. So at Jonah's bidding, they did what they thought best to calm the seas and threw Jonah overboard. The storm stopped, and the sailors offered prayers and vows to the Lord that Jonah served. (See Jonah 1:3-16.)

JUDAS'S REPLACEMENT

The 12 apostles had lost one of their number when their former comrade, Judas, betrayed Christ and then killed himself. They decided to choose a replacement in accordance with Scripture: "Let his position be given to someone else" (Psalm 109:8). Two men were nominated: Joseph called Barsabbas (also known as Justus) and Matthias. They prayed to God to show them who should be chosen and then cast lots. The lot fell to Matthias, who took Judas's place. Ironically, Matthias's name does not appear in Scripture again. (See Acts 1:20-26.)

STRANGE BUT TRUE

The Prophet's Parable

A moving story brings a haughty king to repentance

"You are that man!" The prophet underscored each of the four words with equal emphasis while pointing his bony index finger toward the king's chest. David's face blanched with fear as he swallowed hard. His heart pounded. Full of guilt, he fell on his face in abject repentance. It was a strange reaction indeed from a man who just minutes before had pronounced a self-righteous judgment on a fictitious villain.

David's day began like most other days. The king kissed his wife and newborn son good-bye as he left for the throne room to welcome guests. His secretary informed him that among those he would see that day was a fearless prophet. David had not seen Nathan for a long while, but then again, David had wanted it that way. His conscience had been bothering him since his affair with Bathsheba, a young married woman whose husband had subsequently died. David was not sure how many people knew the sordid details of his adulterous liaison and the cover-up that followed. He hoped Nathan was not among those who had heard the palace gossip.

As Nathan was announced, David was not prepared for the prophet's greeting. "I have a story I'd like to tell you," Nathan began. He proceeded to tell the attentive king of Israel about two men. One was wealthy, the other extremely poor. The poor man and his family owned a pet lamb that was loved and treated as a member of the family. He even sat in the father's lap at mealtime to eat scraps from the table. The rich man owned herds of livestock, but when preparing for the visit of an out-of-town guest, he seized the poor man's lamb and slaughtered it for the evening meal.

The king, himself a shepherd, was incensed to hear of this purported injustice. He interrupted Nathan, calling for the wealthy man to be harshly judged. It was at that point that the steely-eyed prophet stared straight at the king and announced, "You are that man!"

At once David's attempt to rationalize his year-old sin collapsed like a house of cards. Nathan's story was no longer a curious tale; it was a parable with the reflective power of a mirror. The woman the king had viewed from his rooftop lanai was indeed the wife of a man less wealthy and influential than he. David had wives and concubines. The woman's husband claimed but one companion. Still, David had given in to his lust and seduced Bathsheba. Upon hearing of her being pregnant with his child, he arranged for the murder of her soldier-husband.

Uriah's death was not the only fatality in this strange episode in the life of this individual known as "the man after God's own heart." After Nathan confronted David, the child conceived in the king's tryst with Bathsheba died as well.

How is it that David could not have seen the parallel in the prophet's story without the tag line at the end? How could David have lived with himself for over a year knowing he had sinned against his God? Adultery was only one offense. Cover-up and first-degree murder were charges that rendered his moral credit overdrawn. Yet David prayed humbly for forgiveness, and his genuine repentance showed why he was called "a man after God's own heart."

Explore the issue for yourself in 2 Samuel 11:1–12:11. David's prayer of confession and restoration that resulted from his confrontation with Nathan appears as Psalm 51.

FAMINE AND HUNGER

Famine is not just a modern-day phenomenon. The harshness of hunger existed during Bible times too. The book of Jeremiah wins the prize for the most mention of famine or the threat of famine.

Prophet	Affected area	Circumstances	Reference
Agabus	the entire Roman world	Predicted a severe famine that would happen throughout the world during the reign of Claudius.	Acts 11:28
none	Canaan	Abram went to Egypt because of famine.	Genesis 12:9-10
David	Israel	Israel suffered a three-year famine. It was a divine judgment because Saul, the previous king, had persecuted the Gibeonites.	2 Samuel 21:1
Elijah	Israel	Sent to King Ahab to predict that there would be no rain on the earth for three years. Consequently, there was a famine in Samaria.	1 Kings 18:2
Elisha	Israel	This prophet ran into famine more than once. During one famine in Samaria, a city was besieged by the Arameans, who ringed the city to starve the people. The city's inhabitants cooked and ate their own children.	2 Kings 4:38; 6:32–8:2
Ezekiel	Israel	The Lord revealed plans to allow the Israelites to experience the destruction of famine and wild beasts because of their disobedience.	Ezekiel 5:8-17

Isaac	Canaan	Had to go to Abimelech because of famine in the land.	Genesis 26:1-3
none	Judah	Naomi, Elimelech, and their two sons moved to Moab because of famine in Judah.	Ruth 1:1
none	post-exile Judah	Famine hit the land, and poor families had to sell themselves into slavery to stay alive.	Nehemiah 5:1-5
Joseph	Egypt and surrounding lands	Pharaoh had a dream of a seven-year famine after seven years of plenty. Because there was food in Egypt, people in other countries traveled there to buy grain.	Genesis 41
Isaiah	city states of Philistia	The prophet Isaiah predicted that famine was coming to destroy the Philistines.	Isaiah 14:28-30
Jeremiah	Jerusalem	King Zedekiah watched Judah endure a severe famine in Jerusalem because of the encircling Babylonian army.	2 Kings 25:1-7; Jeremiah 32:4

KINGS AND JOKERS

Court jesters were a common sight in medieval royal courts. Their humor kept kings, princes, and lords in good spirits. Surprising as it may seem, the prophets of God sometimes employed puzzles and disguises to dramatize their messages to the kings of Israel. These puzzles, however, were not jokes. On the contrary, they exposed the truth in sharp light.

ELISHA'S PUZZLE

When King Jehoash heard that the prophet Elisha was on his death-bed, the king immediately came to seek out his advice. But instead of getting straightforward answers, Elisha prophesied to him in strange riddles. First he had Jehoash shoot an arrow out of an open window. As the arrow soared toward the distant horizon, Elisha shouted, "The Lord's arrow of victory." That was clear enough—a prediction of success. But then Elisha commanded Jehoash to do something strange indeed; he was to strike the ground with the remaining arrows. Jehoash did so: one, two, and three times. Then he stopped and looked up at Elisha. What next?

Elisha grew red-hot with anger. "You should have struck the ground five or six times! Since you have struck the ground only three times, you will defeat Israel's enemies only three times. You will not completely destroy them." Elisha then died, leaving the king puzzling over the strange ritual he had just been a part of. (See 2 Kings 13:14-20.)

AHIJAH'S RIDDLE

A high official of Solomon's court named Jeroboam was walking on the road that led out of Jerusalem. He met a strange-looking man in a bright new cloak. The man stopped right in front of Jeroboam. With one sweeping gesture, he pulled off his cloak with one hand and pulled out a dagger in the other hand. He stared down at Jeroboam and proceeded to slice up his new cloak. Needless to say, Jeroboam was quite startled. He didn't know if he had run into a bandit or a madman. Then the man spoke: "Take ten pieces of this cloak. God is going to tear ten tribes from Solomon and give them to you. This is God's judgment on Solomon, for he has not followed the Lord as he should." Jeroboam quickly gathered up the ten scraps of clothing. As the prophet predicted, the kingdom of Israel soon split into warring factions. (See 1 Kings 11:29-40; for the prophecy's fulfillment, see 1 Kings 12:20.)

A PROPHET IN DISGUISE

No one could understand the wandering prophet's strange command, "Strike me with your sword." A soldier refused the bizarre request. The prophet rewarded his refusal with a dire prediction of the soldier's death: a lion would maul him. The second man who was given the same command didn't hesitate. He promptly struck the prophet.

The prophet bandaged his wound with a large handkerchief that covered his face. Disguised in this fashion, he waited on the side of a dusty road. When King Ahab approached, the prophet yelled out a disjointed tale. He claimed he had inadvertently allowed a prisoner to slip away. Because of his negligence, he was being required to pay with his own life. What was the king's verdict? Ahab's judgment was severe: the prophet would have to die for his mistake. At this point, the prophet ripped off his disguise and announced God's judgment on Ahab. The king's verdict would fall on his own head, for he had let a prisoner—the king of Syria, the one whom God had condemned—go free. (See 1 Kings 20:23-43.)

CONFIRMED PROPHETIC PREDICTIONS

Every tabloid seems to proclaim bold predictions about the future of popular figures. But while prophetic statements remain as popular as ever in our culture, few "prophets" today would readily submit to the tests of prophecy that God demanded. Any prophet who claimed a source for knowledge other than God or who proved by error not to be a real prophet from God was to be killed (Deuteronomy 18:20). God-given prophecies were to be marked by precise fulfillment. The following chart includes a sample of biblical prophecies and their fulfillment:

Prophecy	Prophet	Reference	Fulfillment
A great nation would come from one's family, eventually blessing the whole world.	God gave this prophecy to Abraham when he invited the patriarch to leave home and trust God.	*Genesis 12:1-2*	By the time Israel arrived in the Promised Land, they had become a great nation (Numbers 23:10). The ongoing, miraculous survival of the Jewish nation bears tribute to God's integrity.
God gave Canaan to Israel as a permanent inheritance.	God gave this promise to Abraham when he returned to Canaan after a brief visit to Egypt.	*Genesis 13:15*	The invasion and conquest of the Promised Land under Joshua (Joshua 21:43-45) established that ownership.
A childless woman's humble prayer would be answered.	A priest named Eli uttered this prophecy without actually knowing the content of Hannah's prayer.	*1 Samuel 1:9-28*	Israel's great prophet, priest, and judge Samuel was born.

The powerful general Sisera would be defeated by a woman.	Deborah the judge delivered this prophecy to Barak because he wouldn't take her word that God would lead the Israelites to victory over Sisera.	Judges 4:1-23	Jael, the wife of Heber, offered Sisera a hiding place in their tent, but when the general was sleeping, she drove a tent peg through his temple.
A childless woman from Shunem would bear a son in a year.	The prophet Elisha gave this prophecy as an expression of gratitude for the unselfish hospitality that the woman's family had extended to him.	2 Kings 4:8-17	The woman gave birth to a son.
Though besieged and starving, the city of Samaria was promised abundant food within 24 hours.	Elisha gave this prophecy to King Joram during a siege of Samaria by King Ben-hadad of Aram.	2 Kings 6:24–7:20	Four desperate lepers ventured out of the city in hopes of begging some food from the Arameans or of being killed. They discovered the well-stocked camp abandoned by an army that had panicked and fled, thinking they were under attack. They left behind an abundant supply of food, which fulfilled the prophecy.
When the promised Savior comes, his own people will reject him.	Isaiah prophesied Jesus' suffering and death hundreds of years before Christ was born.	Isaiah 53:1-9	The people in Israel reject Christ (Luke 23:13-25).

Prophecy	Explanation	Reference	Note
The Messiah will be born in Bethlehem in Judea.	Micah gave the exact location where the promised Savior would be born.	*Micah 5:2; Matthew 2:1-12; Luke 2:1-7*	Note the circumstances recorded in the Gospels (i.e., a Roman emperor imposing a tax that required all to return to their ancestral homes), which ensured the fulfillment of this prophecy.
The powerful and proud city of Nineveh in Assyria (present-day Iraq) would be completely destroyed.	Nahum gave this prophecy almost 50 years before the event, when Assyria appeared invincible.	*Nahum 1:1-3:19*	Nineveh was defeated and destroyed by the Medes in 612 B.C.
The beautiful city of Jerusalem would be destroyed by rampart-building forces who would "not leave a single stone in place."	Jesus gave this prophecy during his last visit to Jerusalem.	*Luke 19:41-44*	Though the Romans had conquered Israel, long before they decided to wipe out Jerusalem as a rebellious outpost in A.D. 70, some 40 years after Jesus' death and resurrection.
A disciple would deny knowing Jesus.	Jesus predicted Peter's denial during the last supper with his disciples the night before his crucifixion. Peter vehemently protested.	*John 18:25-27*	After Jesus' arrest, in the courtyard of the high priest, Peter denied knowing Jesus three times.

How the Mighty Have Fallen

What accounts for the mental breakdown of King Nebuchadnezzar?

One brilliant day, the powerful and mighty King Nebuchadnezzar stood on the roof of his expansive palace and surveyed his empire—his beautiful gardens, his magnificent temples, his luxurious palaces. All the people from throughout the entire ancient world were his subjects and in his service. His heart swelled with pride. This was the kingdom he had built; this was the city he had constructed. It was the crown of his life, full of his great achievements.

As he strolled on the palace roof, a prediction that had been pronounced by a Jewish advisor a year earlier came to pass. Nebuchadnezzar's sanity escaped him; his mind became confused. He went mad, rushing to and fro.

His lifestyle quickly deteriorated. Instead of eating the best food and drinking the best wine of the empire, Nebuchadnezzar began gobbling down whatever he could get his hands on. He began living like an animal—even stooping to eating grass. His own servants couldn't stand to wait on him or take care of him. He was uncontrollable. And eventually Nebuchadnezzar, the great king of Babylon, was driven from his own people to live in the fields like a common beast. No one took care of him. No one trimmed his hair or even his fingernails. He had gone completely insane.

What was the cause of his sudden calamity? Why such a complete reversal of fortunes? The entire kingdom of Babylon marveled at their king, who was now wallowing in the fields. But a quiet Jew named Daniel claimed to know the cause of the king's sudden insanity.

Daniel told the peculiar story of a restless night that King Nebuchadnezzar had endured. The king had been troubled by a disturbing dream—a very disturbing dream about an enormous tree. The tree was so large that all creatures were able to find shelter beneath it; its fruit was so abundant that all creatures were able to be fed by it. Suddenly an angel appeared in the dream and ordered the tree to be cut down and its branches and fruit stripped. The angel then announced that an unidentified person would be forced to live like an animal for seven years.

The dream unsettled Nebuchadnezzar. He called for his advisors, including the pensive Daniel. The meaning of the dream became clear to Daniel. Both the tree and the unidentified "him" referred to by the angel were Nebuchadnezzar himself. Like the tree, the king had become great and powerful. His kingdom encompassed most of the known world. Yet because the king refused to acknowledge the divine source of his power, Nebuchadnezzar would be "cut down to size." His kingdom would be taken away from him for seven years. During that time, the great king Nebuchadnezzar would become like an animal, eating grass and living in the fields. A year later, Daniel's prediction came true with startling accuracy.

But Nebuchadnezzar's disturbance had a happy ending. Eventually, he came to realize the cause of his madness and humbled himself before God. As his sanity returned, the king reassumed his responsibilities. He offered a prayer of thanks to God, whom he acknowledged as "the King of heaven."

For more information on Nebuchadnezzar's insanity and his eventual recovery, see Daniel 4.

 ## ABUSED PROPHETS AND PROPHETESSES

Battered, beaten, and beheaded—being a messenger for God was no easy task, especially when your message was an unwelcome one. Here is what some of God's spokespersons endured.

1. The prophet Elisha was teased for having a bald head (2 Kings 2:23-24).
2. Hanani was jailed for rebuking King Asa's sin (2 Chronicles 16:7-10).
3. The prophet Uriah was hacked to death with a sword and buried in an unmarked grave for speaking out against Judah's sin (Jeremiah 26:20-23).

4. John the Baptist was beheaded after Herodias's daughter requested his head on a tray (Matthew 14:6-8).
5. The prophet Jeremiah was jailed and then thrown into a muddy hole in the ground for predicting the fall of Jerusalem (Jeremiah 31:1–38:13).
6. The prophet Jonah was tossed into the sea, swallowed by a large fish, and spit back out onto shore (Jonah 1:4–2:10).
7. After rebelling against God, Miriam was stricken with leprosy (Numbers 12:9-15).
8. The prophet Micaiah was slapped, arrested, put in jail, and fed only enough bread and water to keep him alive after he gave evil King Ahab unwanted news (1 Kings 22:8-28; 2 Chronicles 18:12-26).
9. Queen Jezebel wanted to kill all of God's prophets. One hundred of them fled to two caves to hide and subsist on bread and water (1 Kings 18:3-4).
10. After winning his contest with the evil prophets and destroying them, the prophet Elijah fled for his life to the wilderness, where he prayed that God would let him die (1 Kings 19:1-3).
11. The prophet Zechariah was executed in the court of the Temple after confronting the people of Judah for ignoring God (2 Chronicles 24:20-22).

CURIOUS CONNECTIONS

SIGNS AND SHADOWS

God gave signs and miracles to his people to draw them to himself. The Bible tells of many mysterious events and phenomena far beyond human capability to understand. To read the signs required more than intellectual discernment—it demanded a love and respect for God.

THE DAY A SHADOW MOVED BACKWARD

When the prophet Isaiah told King Hezekiah that God would heal his illness, the king was doubtful and asked for a sign from God.

Isaiah agreed and asked the king whether he wanted to see the shadow on the sundial go forward ten points or backward ten points. "The shadow always moves forward," Hezekiah said. "Make it go backward." So Isaiah asked God to make the shadow on the sundial move backward ten points . . . and it did! Hezekiah recovered from his near-fatal illness to live another fifteen years. (See 2 Kings 20:1-11.)

THE RAINBOW

When Noah stepped off the ark, he entered a new world. All previous life had been wiped out by the calamitous flood that covered the earth for months and months. Noah's first gesture was to offer a sacrifice of thanks to God for sparing him and his family. God responded to that offering by making his first covenant with humankind. He promised to never destroy the earth again by flood. To give an everlasting sign of that promise, he set a rainbow in the sky—a beautiful, heavenly, and tangible reminder of his love for all people and all creatures on earth. (See Genesis 8:20–9:17.)

THE VOICE

Jesus always told his disciples and the crowds that came to hear him that the miracles he performed were for their benefit. These signs confirmed that Jesus came from God. They also reinforced the faith of those who believed or who were struggling with their faith. (Consequently, Jesus did not perform signs for the hard-hearted or the disbelieving; see Matthew 12:38-42; Mark 6:5-6.) As Jesus neared the time of his death, he spoke to a crowd about the trials he would suffer and concluded, "Father, bring glory to your name." A voice from heaven declared, "I have already brought it glory, and I will do it again." The crowd, astonished by what they heard, debated its source. Some thought it was thunder, while others thought they had heard an angel. Jesus then told them the voice was for their benefit, not his. After admonishing them to walk in the light before the darkness came, Jesus left them. (See John 12:28-36.)

The Deception

A father's blessing and curse that couldn't be undone

"Why . . . why can't you bless me?!" The loud cry pierced the silence. "Bless me. . . . Bless me too," came the anxious plea again. The wrinkled and gray old man was sitting straight up, a troubled look on his face. His son, a livid young man named Esau, was pacing back and forth in the tent. "Please bless me, Father," he cried. "Please bless me." Isaac stared straight ahead, seemingly unaffected by the commotion. Blind for many years, Isaac could not see his anguished son, but he certainly could hear his loud pleas.

Finally Isaac spoke. "Your brother was here, and he tricked me. He has carried away your blessing. I have made Jacob your master and have declared that all his brothers will be his servants. I have guaranteed him an abundance of grain and wine. What is there left to give to you?"

Esau collapsed, weeping bitterly. "Not one blessing left for me?" As Esau sobbed, his face buried in his hands, Isaac slowly stretched out his bony hand and placed it on his son's head. In quiet monotones, Isaac pronounced, "You will live by your sword. You will serve your brother for a time" (Genesis 27:34-40).

These were not the words Esau was looking for. They fell on his ears like pelting rain. His heart sank. His stomach churned. Finally he stormed out of the tent, vowing to kill his brother, Jacob. That brother of his had stolen his blessing and left him with his father's curse.

How could the words of a feeble old man hold so much power? Why couldn't Isaac take his blessing back from his conniving younger son, Jacob? How could mere words change the destinies of these two young men: Esau and his brother, Jacob?

Isaac's curse did come true. King David, a descendant of Jacob, conquered the Edomites, Esau's descendants, around 1000 B.C. For centuries after that, the Edomites lived to the south of Israel in a desert region under Israel's dominion (2 Samuel 8:14).

Why did Isaac's words hold so much power? The ancients

believed that a spoken curse contained inherent power to accomplish itself. This explains Esau's reaction. But it does not explain why Isaac's words came true or why Isaac couldn't take his blessing back. Could Isaac, although physically blind, see centuries into the future? Did Isaac hold the future of his sons in his wrinkled hands?

The key to this mystery lay in the heart of Rebekah, Isaac's wife. Decades before, she had buried a secret deep within herself. When she was a young woman pregnant with twins, her days and nights had been filled with great pain. The two babies in her womb were continually struggling, kicking, and fighting. The pain kept her up late into the cool desert nights and filled her days with agony. Finally, in desperation, she sought out a place to be alone. There, she poured out her grief to the God of Abraham. Why this pain? Why her?

God spoke to her: "The sons in your womb will become two rival nations. One nation will be stronger than the other; the descendants of your older son will serve the descendants of your younger son" (Genesis 25:23).

It was obvious to Rebekah that God had predicted Jacob's and Esau's fate long before their father had pronounced his words of blessing and condemnation. Isaac's dying words did not hold any power over her sons' lives; God had determined the destinies of her two sons long before.

For more on this story, read Genesis 27.

DID YOU KNOW?

Urim and Thummim

Did you know that the ancient high priests of Israel used Urim and Thummim to receive direct revelations from God (Numbers 27:21)? How the high priest received these revelations and what the Urim and Thummim actually were remains a mystery buried in the ancient past. All that is known for certain is that the Urim and Thummim are connected with the breastplate worn by the high priest (Exodus 28:30). On this breastplate were 12 precious stones engraved with the names of each one of the 12 tribes of Israel.

Some have suggested that these 12 stones were in fact the Urim and Thummim, but many biblical commentators believe that the Urim and Thummim were gems kept in a pouch over the high priest's heart. Some believe these gems were engraved with some symbol that reflected a yes, no, or divine silence (1 Samuel 28:6). Other commentators have suggested that the high priest received revelations by observing some type of mysterious light reflected by these gems. The details concerning Urim and Thummim remain a mystery because their use decreased after King David's reign. After that, Israel's prophets revealed God's will to the people.

STRANGE BUT TRUE

Desert Visitors

Who were the mysterious travelers who told Abraham about future events?

The sun shone high one hot afternoon in ancient Canaan. Three dusty travelers slowly approached several tents that had been placed amidst a pleasant oak grove. These were Abraham's tents, and his family lived among these oak trees at Mamre. They didn't receive many visitors. So when Abraham saw the three approaching, he encouraged his wife, Sarah, to prepare a meal. They had to stop here, he thought; they had to stay with him for a while and tell him the news of far-off places.

Abraham exchanged the usual greetings with the strangers. Although he did not recognize their faces, for some reason he kept having an odd feeling that he knew these men from somewhere. The three agreed to stay. Abraham was delighted.

After a hearty meal, the men started on their way. They were heading to Sodom. Since Abraham knew the way well—his nephew Lot lived there—he accompanied the men. As they walked, the talk of these three grew strange. One spoke of the city of Sodom with great displeasure. He had heard of the evil that thrived in that city—unspeakable perversions. He even spoke of destroying the city because of its wickedness.

Abraham—by now he knew his visitors were angels, perhaps even God himself—pleaded with the man to spare the city if only 10 righteous persons could be found there. The man agreed. And Abraham returned home, never to see the mysterious trio again.

But the next day, Sodom was a smoldering ash heap. Had the man's armies come and destroyed it? Had the trio sabotaged the city by torching it in the middle of the night?

These were all plausible explanations for the sudden destruction of a thriving city. But the villagers of the nearby towns told a far different story. They spoke of a great ball of fire and sulfur raining down on the city, licking up all its inhabitants—save one man and his daughters. The one man who had barely escaped this appalling plight was Abraham's nephew Lot. Filled with great fear, Lot lived the rest of his days in the caves of the region.

The tale Lot told of that harrowing night filled listeners with dread. He told of two visitors who insisted that he leave his hometown that instant. That night, a raucous party filled Sodom's streets. But Lot and his family were forced to ignore the revelry because of the strangers' passionate pleas. They had to leave. So they did, only to barely escape the hot sulfur that rained down from the night sky. His wife, who was with him, stole a quick look back and, with that glance, lost her life.

We may never know with complete certainty whom Abraham hosted on that hot day. But given the sudden fiery destruction of Sodom and nearby Gomorrah—by means unavailable to ancients—we may have to accept, as Abraham did, that his visitors were from another realm.

For more on Abraham's visitors and the subsequent destruction of Sodom, read Genesis 18–19.

HEARING VOICES

All of the people in the following chart claim they heard voices or divine messages. Skeptics still may discount these stories as hallucinations, but how does one explain voices heard by crowds? Read on to discover the circumstances behind these mysterious voices.

Hearer	Circumstances / Reference
The apostle John	Heard a loud voice that sounded like a trumpet. It told him to write down everything he saw. *Revelation 1:10-11*
King Nebuchadnezzar	In a dream, heard an angel's voice that told him to cut down a tree. *Daniel 4:13-14*
Jesus, John the Baptist, and crowds	At Jesus' baptism, the crowd heard a voice from heaven saying, "This is my beloved Son, and I am fully pleased with him." *Matthew 3:16-17*
Young Samuel	Samuel was asleep in the Temple when he heard a voice calling him three times. He thought it was Eli, the priest, but finally he realized it was God who was speaking. *1 Samuel 3:1-14*
Elijah	After fleeing for his life from Queen Jezebel, Elijah heard God's voice telling him to go back to Damascus and anoint three people. *1 Kings 19:13-16*
John	Heard an eagle loudly calling, "Terror, terror, terror to all who belong to this world because of what will happen." *Revelation 8:13*
Saul	Saul was on his way to Damascus to persecute Christians, when a dazzling light shone on him and he heard the voice of Jesus. *Acts 9:1-6*
Peter	The apostle saw the sky open and saw a sheet suspended by its four corners and filled with animals, snakes, and birds (forbidden food for the Jews). He then heard a voice telling him it was all right to eat these things. *Acts 10:9-21*
Balaam	Balaam's donkey spoke to him and rebuked him for his greediness and evildoing. *2 Peter 2:15-16*
Jesus, Peter, James, and John	The three disciples were with Jesus when his appearance changed and his face and clothes shone. Then a bright cloud appeared and a voice said, "This is my beloved Son, and I am fully pleased with him. Listen to him." *Matthew 17:1-5*

Mountains of Blessings, Mountains of Curses

A great prophet's dying command

Wizened and thin, the aged Moses spoke to the assembled tribes of Israel. His voice, though noticeably weaker, still resonated with the authority he had possessed for decades. Earlier he had summoned the people of Israel to this great gathering. They knew something of great importance was going to happen—but what? Adding to the drama was the army of followers that stood with Moses. For the first time ever, the elders of Israel had joined Moses publicly as he addressed the nation.

Moses had scant time to finish his work on earth. Nearly 120 years old, he knew that he would not be with his people when they entered the Promised Land. Yet he feared that they would tend to slide into disobedience as they often had during their 40-year trek through the desert. So he instructed the people to remember God in the new land by going through an elaborate—and somewhat mysterious—ceremony.

Once the people crossed the Jordan and entered the Promised Land, they were to pause and remember God's words. To do this, they were to place large stones on Mount Ebal and coat them with plaster. The leaders were to write the law (most likely the key points) on the stones as a visible reminder of God's demands for a holy life. After the stones had been set up, the people would feast and offer sacrifices.

When the feasting was over, a great ceremony would mark the inheritance of the new land. Moses instructed the tribes to assemble near two mountains once they had crossed the Jordan. The tribes of Simeon, Levi, Judah, Issachar, Joseph, and Benjamin would gather at the foot of Mount Gerizim and announce blessings to the people, while the tribes of Reuben, Gad, Asher, Zebulun, Dan, and Naphtali would meet in front of Mount Ebal and declare curses to those who violated God's law. The physical setting lent itself well to the messages: Ebal was barren and craggy, but Gerizim, just south of Ebal, was covered in trees and rich vegetation.

Standing between the tribes in the rich valley of Shechem below, Moses instructed the Levites, the priestly caretakers and spiritual leaders of the nation, to lead the people in this great act of remembrance. They were to recite a series of curses intended for those who disobeyed: twelve in all, symbolic perhaps of the twelve tribes of Israel. Yet for those who followed the law, God promised blessing. The people would harvest abundant crops, keep enemies at bay, and remain prosperous. Their covenant would testify to the love of God, and the neighboring peoples would stand in awe of them (Deuteronomy 28:10).

After Moses finished his instructions, he presented Joshua as Israel's new leader. A short time later Moses died, having glimpsed from a mountain peak the land he would never enter. But would the people of Israel take to heart his parting words?

In fact, they did. After the Israelites had defeated the Canaanite strongholds of Jericho and Ai, Joshua called for a great assembly of Israel in the place Moses had specified. The great stones of the altar were piled up, and Joshua copied the law onto the stones. Then in what must have been an awe-inspiring sight, six tribes assembled before Mount Gerizim and the others in front of Ebal. Between them marched the Levites, holding the Ark of the Covenant. Joshua read the blessings and curses to the entire assembly, and they affirmed each word with a ringing "Amen!" So the dying words of Moses were fulfilled.

Spectacular as it must have been, the ceremony of the blessings and curses had one simple objective: to impress upon the Israelites the importance of their covenant with God. As the people would discover in the lawless period of the judges that followed Joshua's death, curses did follow in the wake of sin; only when they remembered God and turned to him were they saved from their plight.

To read more about the ceremony of blessings and curses, read Deuteronomy 27–28. To learn how Joshua fulfilled Moses' command, read Joshua 8:30-35.

PROPHECIES

Is prophecy just another name for fortune-telling?

Prophecy involves much more than foretelling events. Prophets were God's spokespersons, just as Aaron was a spokesman for Moses (Exodus 7:1-2). Prophets' words were God's words (for example, Jonah 1:1).

Many of the prophecies in the Bible are conditional, depending on the response of those who hear the prophecy. If the people turned to God, the prophets would predict peace and God's lavish blessings. If the people stubbornly persisted in sin, the prophets would predict suffering and destruction (Deuteronomy 30:15-18). In addition to this basic message of repentance, prophets of the Bible did predict the future. In many cases, these prophecies spoke of a coming Savior who would deliver God's people and described the eventual defeat of all wickedness (Micah 7:7-10). In a few cases, time periods (Daniel 9:24-27), specific locations (such as Bethlehem for Jesus' birth in Micah 5:2), and specific names (Cyrus in Isaiah 45:2) are mentioned in Bible prophecies. But in general, the prophet's message was a consistent and clear call for repentance.

How should I respond to those who claim they have a message directly from God?

Not everyone who claims to be a prophet speaks for God. All of us must test a prophet to see if he or she speaks the truth. The first test for a prophet is Scripture. God never contradicts himself. If someone says something that is against the Bible, then that person is a false prophet. The Bible clearly states that if a prophet encourages people to worship a god other than the God of Israel, then that person is a deceiver (Deuteronomy 13:1-3). The second test for a prophet is whether the prophet's predictions come true. If a prophet predicts a certain date for some event and that date passes without it coming true, then that prophet is a false prophet (Deuteronomy 18:21-22). There will always be people who claim to speak for God. It takes careful discernment to know whom to listen to and whom to ignore.

Should I believe anyone who claims to know when Jesus is coming back to the earth?
Just as no one knows when an accident will occur—it always happens unexpectedly (Ecclesiastes 9:12)—so no one knows when the world will end. Not even the angels know when God will end history as we know it (Matthew 24:36). The Bible says that false prophets claiming to be God will try to deceive people (Matthew 24:24-28). But no one should believe those who claim to be God. When God comes to this earth, all will know with certainty that he is God. His arrival will be announced with a loud trumpet call, and God will appear so that all can see his glory (Matthew 24:27-31). God will come, and his coming will be unmistakable. The Bible warns us to make sure we are prepared for his coming (Matthew 24:42, 44; Luke 12:40).